OTHER BOOKS AND AUDIO BOOKS

BY CHRISTIE GARDINER

You Are the Mother Your Children Need

Our Family Christmas

HOLY
as you are

Seeking

Divine Moments

in Your

Ordinary

Extraordinary

Life

From the best-selling author of
You Are the Mother Your Children Need

CHRISTIE GARDINER

Covenant Communications, Inc.

For the little girl in all of us

She dreamed big dreams, fought big fights, slayed big dragons, and knew that in spite of everything, she was a daughter of God, who loved her. The faith of our younger selves made us *holy as we are*. If these little girls only knew how thankful we, their grown-up versions, are for them.

For Hailey and Elisabeth
and Jordan, Annaka, Kathleen, Annie, Ella, and Goldie

Dream big, my girls, dream big.
"I don't think any change in the world has been more significant than the change in the status of women. At the time the Relief Society was founded, a woman's world was her home, her family, and perhaps a little community service. Today a woman's world is as broad as the universe. There's scarcely an area of human endeavor that a woman cannot enter if she has the will and preparation to do so."[1]

For Christian

I'll be loving you, buddy, "*Always.*"

And for Doug,

my love.
"If ever two were one then surely we. If ever man were loved by wife, then thee."[2]

1 Belle Spafford, Relief Society General President. "Reaching Every Facet of a Woman's Life," Ensign, June 1974.
2 Anne Bradstreet, *To my Dear and Loving Husband,* 1612.

Preface

a letter: hey, sis, it's me.

"Our stories are what make the difference, and if we can tell them honestly we can hope to help each other. In the end, we have nothing to offer each other but our stories."

—Emma Lou Thayne

Hey, sis, it's me.

It's been a couple of years since we've talked, and I've missed it. I think about you all the time—even those of you who are new to our little tribe. I'm so excited for you to join us. Sisters, the stories you've told me these past couple years . . . well, they've changed me. If I have learned anything from having met you, it is that we are more the same than different. We really are sisters.

I pray for you.

I pray for Jennifer and her kids as she struggles in spite of past mistakes to know that the Atonement makes it possible for her to be the mother her children need. The theatre-loving Ariel, my little sister, I pray for you; the sweet teenage girl who comes to my events and makes me smile, who reads my books even though we are separated by years! Emilee, a talented crafting artist who is an awesome mother to her children, one of whom has different abilities, is in my prayers often.

And on and on and on. I pray for and care about all of you—the women I've met and the ones I haven't yet. I pray because, well, we are sisters. Hearing your stories has allowed me to be a witness to your amazing, challenging lives, just as in reading my books, you have been a witness to mine. Everyone needs a witness. I know that each one of the stories you've told me represents the story of thousands of women in our global Relief Society sisterhood of 7.1 million.[3] Nothing can separate us from each other; we are all one in Christ. Please know that the experiences I've had meeting you, hearing what you've had to say, and looking into your eyes have been holy, sacred moments in my life. In a world that values sharing filtered perfection, thanks for being brave enough to share your real self with me. I saw you and you were . . . are beautiful.

I love you. And above all, I know you are divinely loved by Heavenly Parents whose love is infinite and perfect. That is why I write. To remind you (and me) of what we already know: we belong.

New friends and old, thanks for finding your way to this new conversation about holiness. I can't wait to see and hear from you again and to discuss what you've learned about what happens when we choose to live a holy life. We're blessed by our shared sisterhood. Let's talk soon.

Love,
Christie

---

3 https://www.lds.org/church/news/relief-society-to-celebrate-175-years-in-2017?lang=eng&_r=1; accessed November 11, 2018.

"*It is the duty of each one of us to be a holy woman. We shall have elevated aims, if we are holy women. We shall feel that we are called to perform important duties. No one is exempt from them. There is no sister so isolated, and her sphere so narrow but what she can do a great deal towards establishing the Kingdom of God upon the earth.*"[4]

—Eliza R. Snow

4 "An Address," *Woman's Exponent*, Sept. 15, 1873, 62.

Introduction
seeking and choosing a holy life

"Ask, and it shall be given you; seek, and ye shall find; knock, and it shall be opened unto you. For every one that asketh receiveth; and he that seeketh findeth; and to him that knocketh it shall be opened."

—Luke 11:9–10

What do you think about your life as it is? What do you want most? For me, that answer is easy. I want a *holy* life. I crave it. But what is it exactly? Sometimes, the real meaning of the word *holy* gets lost. I'm not talking about wanting a sanctimonious kind of life that appears to be somehow elevated as I look down my nose in mocking piety at others. And I definitely don't want a life where I sit atop holiness, just skimming its surface on Sundays when my neighbors are looking. A life of holiness in its true definition is what I'm looking for. The supplementary materials in scripture tell us that "things or places [are] holy that [are] set apart for a sacred purpose."[5] That's the definition of a life I want to live, one I set apart as sacred in any way I can—day after day—before finally laying it all before Christ at the end of my days.

---

5 Bible Dictionary, "Holiness."

The ache to become authentically holy is deep and real. I want nothing to do with a holy life that comes from the outside or is informed by other people's expectations of me. I'm tired of listening to them! No, I want holiness from the inside out, a life that is holy because I chose to set it apart from the world.

If God could hold a rope of light, throw it down, and tie it around my heart, and if I could just walk around my whole life like that, tethered to heaven no matter where I went; and if that rope were so strong that even my life's biggest storms couldn't break it; and if, when my sin severed it, I let my Elder Brother trim the frayed ends and tie me back to it; and even if living life like this took me a little bit apart from most of the world, maybe even made me peculiar, it would be okay because that is the life I want—a life lassoed in light around the heart of heaven.

After talking with so many of you over the past years, it is clear to me that we all have more in common than not. We are insatiably hungry for divine connection. And I thought that maybe you might be looking for an element of holiness too. Are you?

The words on these pages are the things I've learned as I've sought in earnest to create a life set apart from the world for a sacred purpose. Thoughts within will address what living a life of holiness means; how to find holiness in character, habits, relationships, and attributes; methods for infusing holiness into ordinary daily tasks; and even ways to overcome some of the biggest obstacles in seeking a life of holiness.

I don't back away from life's hard things in this book. I tried not to touch them, but I failed. Real life kept coming back to my thoughts. I made some of my most significant discoveries as I asked myself questions like: Can I have a holy life if I hold questions and faith at the same time? Can holiness be found in spite of my suffering or even within it? What does a holy life look like for a woman in Christ's Church?

> Holiness is found in seeking it and in choosing it.

The most important thing I've discovered is that holiness is found in seeking it and in choosing it. When I search for holy moments, I find them, and the choice to see my life as holy is available to me in any moment of every day, no matter what is or isn't happening.

I love sharing my favorite things with my friends, and because you are my friends, I want to share the possibility and hope of this idea with you. If you search for holy moments and if you choose them, you can experience the bliss of holiness every day!

I have to tell you one little thing before you jump into chapter one: I'm not qualified to write this book. There. I've said it. Now you know and can proceed at your own risk. I have this silly idea that if I tell you the truth of what I know about myself, it won't be awkward for either of us. My husband hates this about me because, in actuality, it makes things a lot more awkward for everyone involved. But I think it's important to let you know I am not qualified to write this book.

My lack of qualifications was brought to my attention at my very first book signing. Upon arrival at the signing, I was thrilled to see a line out the door and down the shopping complex.

What I didn't understand at first was that I was signing with the legendary Hank Smith. No one was there to see me; I was just the person at the table they had to pass on the way to Hank. And who can blame them; he's not only hilarious but very smart and extremely kind.

The cool, confident ice I had tried to form around myself to protect me from my fear of rejection quickly broke. All the confidence I had mustered that morning was stripped away, and my vulnerabilities came floating to the surface. (It might be scary when this happens to us, but as scary as it is, vulnerability is real. And real is where the good stuff is. It's where we can connect.) By the time the patrons got to my table at the signing, they had been waiting the better part of an hour and still had a five-minute wait for Hank. One by one, they awkwardly passed me, holding their stacks of Hank's products while politely feigning interest in my book or looking up as if all the mysteries of the universe could be explained by staring at the shapes of the popcorn ceiling.

At one point, an impatient and exasperated woman picked up my book (a book about motherhood), opened it, read for a minute, shut it with a loud snap, slammed it back down on the table in what appeared to be total disgust, and with a loud voice asked, "What makes you think you're qualified to write a book about motherhood anyway?"

The crowd around my little table hushed, and everyone looked at me.

I burst out laughing. I couldn't help it. "Nothing," I said. "Absolutely nothing qualifies me to write this book. What would qualify anyone to write this book? Which is exactly why I had to write it."

She bought two copies. And no, she did not have me sign them.

The same lack of qualifications applies to this book about holiness. It feels hypocritical to write it, to pretend that I even understand what it means to lead a holy life, let alone implement the practices required to attain one. I am inadequate, but who but Christ wouldn't be?

In 2002, President Eyring spoke about callings in general conference. He said, "There will be times when you will feel overwhelmed. One of the ways you will be attacked is with the feeling that you are inadequate. Well, *you are inadequate* to answer a call to represent God with only your own powers. But you have access to more than your natural capacities, and you do not work alone."[6]

While writing isn't a calling The Church of Jesus Christ of Latter-day Saints has extended to me, it is my life's work. I feel called to it and know that I do not write alone. I'm inadequate, *and* I'm going to share this book with you anyway because our inadequacies are what keep us needing our Savior and His grace, and I know He can magnify my ideas to influence others for good. He can do the same for you and your life's work.

Although I have felt inspired, these pages aren't doctrine; they're just ideas. And the ideas you have as you read aren't just as valid as mine—your own ideas are *even more valid* because the Spirit is speaking to *you* for *your* life. Sister, when that happens, write those things down. The way I see and understand things is the right way for me, and the way you see and understand is the right way for you.

---

6 Henry B. Eyring. "Rise to Your Call," *Ensign.* November 2002; emphasis added.

And I'll continue to work toward holiness—even and especially—beyond the completion of this book. I imagine that till my earthly life is done and even beyond, I'll be seeking for ways to set myself apart for a sacred purpose. We have all been writing the books of our holy lives since we chose our Savior's plan before coming to this earth. This book is my invitation, challenge, and gift. I give it to you, to myself, and to every woman who has ever wondered what it means to seek a holy life.

The struggle between the ideal of a holy life and the reality of our whirlwind days can seem far apart. I am totally aware of that. (I write, having just cleaned up my child's vomit on the way to a writing retreat.) The words on these pages seek to close the gap, reminding all of us as women of the holy attributes we already possess. Even with our simplest offerings, we can accomplish great and tiny works that will forever change the landscape and heart-scape of the world.

While offering many ideas and new ways of thinking, this book isn't a formula. If you want ten easy steps to living a holy life, this isn't it. There is no one specific formula for a holy life because you and I are not the constants in an equation; we are the variables. No, this book can't give you the secrets that will fix you. But, sis, what if you don't need to be fixed?

I'm going to ask you to get a little bit uncomfortable, to look into your life and be honest with yourself. Look at your tragedies, triumphs, and everything in between as sacred opportunities to choose holiness. Believe me, I know you think you aren't holy. I know you think you're ordinary. But tonight, lying in bed, just before falling asleep, as you look back on your ordinary life, think about all you have done today. If you were

> The efforts you exerted set your
> life apart from the world
> for a sacred purpose.

not a woman of Christ, would what you did today have been the same? If yours were an ordinary life, would you have prayed with your kids before school or before the big presentation in front of your colleagues? And yes, maybe you only read one verse of scripture after falling into bed, but would you have thought to open your scriptures if your heart were not with Him? The discussion that you initiated with the young women at the youth activity didn't prepare itself; wasn't that your effort? When you passed a woman experiencing homelessness on the street, then flipped the car around and gave her the food you just picked up for your family's meal, opting to have a candlelight dinner of PB&J sandwiches with the family instead, weren't you listening to the Spirit's call? Maybe all you did today was get out of bed, get dressed, take one step after another, and make it through the entire day with hope that because of Christ, tomorrow has the possibility of being a better day. Be it one of these or millions of other things you do with Christ in mind, today you are a different woman than most. Whatever your day looks like and in spite of your failures, mistakes, inadequacies, and shortcomings, the efforts you exerted set your life apart from the world for a sacred purpose. Your life is different because you know who you are, and you tried, even if imperfectly, to rise to your station as a daughter of God and a disciple of Christ. "As [you] come to understand who [you] really are—God's daughters, with an innate capacity to love and nurture—[you] reach [your] potential as holy women."[7] What if, because of Jesus Christ and the redemption that comes through His Atonement, your ordinary *is* extraordinary? What if you are *holy as you are?*

---

7 "Live Up to Your Privilege." *Daughters in My Kingdom: The History and Work of Relief Society (2011)*, 169.

Chapter One
holiness of heart

*"O Lord, pour out thy Spirit upon thy [daughter] that [she]
may do this work with holiness of heart."*

—Mosiah 18:12

What is holiness? When referenced in the scriptures, the word *holy* means to "set apart for a sacred purpose." It is a description all of us who seek to follow Christ want to embody.

Alma is one of my favorites. The elder. The younger gets a lot of our attention due to the engaging and redemptive nature of his narrative arc, but the first Alma's story is pretty amazing too! It has all the elements of good storytelling. If you want a definition of *holiness*, you won't find one better than this amazing prophet.

Alma chose a different path from the one he'd planned. There he was, right smack-dab in the middle of a dream life. The scriptures tell us he was a young man and already a priest to the king! Not bad for an ambitious guy full of promise. Then he heard Abinadi, and just like that, everything changed. Abinadi warned the king and his priests of their evil ways. He taught the gospel and encouraged them to repent. A spark of faith in what Abinadi said ignited young Alma's heart to the point that he was willing to give up his secure life of luxury. Looking back on this moment, the voice of the Lord said Alma was "blessed because of [his] exceeding faith in the words alone of my servant Abinadi."[8] But in the moment when Alma had to choose to stay with King Noah or believe Abinadi, there were no certainties, no heavenly assurances that this was the right path. All Alma had to go on was faith. We know what ends up happening to King Noah and his priests (spoiler: Noah is burned at the stake, and his priests become kidnappers and outcasts), but Alma had no way of knowing their grim future. The only things guiding him were the powerful words of a humble missionary and the spark of a testimony he found in them. The spark was enough for him to choose Christ over convenience and walk away (okay, admittedly, he didn't walk; he fled, which he had to do because he'd angered King Noah. He walk-fled away) from his seemingly bright future into the unknown. What was to come for him wasn't easy and wasn't at all what he had planned, but because of his willingness to act on his faith, generations turned toward Christ. For Alma, it was his life's defining moment.

> Each life holds unlimited potential for holy moments.

We all have defining moments when we choose to set our lives apart for a sacred purpose. Each life holds unlimited potential for holy moments. Some of these will be moments of

---

8 Mosiah 26:15.

great significance, like Alma's leaving his entire life behind. And some will be of little worldly consequence but of great eternal consequence in the development and deepening of your soul, like taking time to see the spores on a fern leaf and thinking that these little cases contain all the reproductive material for the fern in their perfect little rows.

I had one of these defining moments when I was eighteen. My life's path was pretty clear in my mind. Having studied and worked as an actress for my entire childhood, there came a time when I had to choose.

The university I was attending asked me to violate my firmly held religious convictions. Upon declining to violate covenants I had made with Heavenly Father, I was told I would be removed from my program.

Like Alma trying to reason with King Noah, in the beginning, I thought that reasoning with the university would help. I thought if I explained my religious conviction, they would see reason. Through the weeks, we went back and forth, but they never did understand that in practicing my religion the way I saw fit for me, I could not do the things they were asking me to do. Over many months, the battle raged, and eventually, like Alma, I was cast out.

Upon being cast out, Alma fled and spent his days hiding from King Noah in a thicket of small trees. There, in hiding, Alma took the time to write "all the words which Abinadi had spoken."[9] He recorded the teachings of the gospel, then went in secret among the people and began to teach as Abinadi had taught him. Many of them began to feel the same spark that had emboldened Alma to set out into his new life. Those who

9 Mosiah 17:4.

believed came to a place called Mormon. It was near the trees and had a fountain of pure water running through it. Here they listened as Alma preached the gospel of repentance, redemption, and faith. It was at these waters that Alma called the people to action with some of the most powerful words. He says,

> As ye are desirous to come into the fold of God and to be called his people, and are willing to bear one another's burdens, that they may be light; Yea, and are willing to mourn with those that mourn; yea, and comfort those that stand in need of comfort, and to stand as witnesses of God at all times and in all things, and in all places that ye may be in, even until death, that ye may be redeemed of God, and be numbered with those of the first resurrection, that ye may have eternal life—Now I say unto you, if this be the desire of your hearts, what have you against being baptized in the name of the Lord, as a witness before him that ye have entered into a covenant with him, that ye will serve him and keep his commandments, that he may pour out his Spirit more abundantly upon you?[10]

The people clapped their hands with joy, exclaiming, "This is the desire of our hearts!"[11] Alma then took Helam into the water to be baptized. Think of it! We read that Alma had authority from the Almighty God to baptize, but we aren't

10 Mosiah 18:8–10.
11 Mosiah 18:11.

told in the scriptures how Alma received this authority. Can you imagine the spiritual communion and personal revelation he must have experienced to know that he had the authority to baptize? What divine communication took place in his hidden thicket? Yet, in spite of knowing he had the authority, it couldn't have been easy to just hop into the water. Helam was the first person Alma baptized. Human nature suggests to my mind that Alma was spiritually secure in his authority but perhaps a little humanly apprehensive as he and Helam walked into the water. The scriptures say Alma said two prayers. First, a prayer for himself, then a long and lovely baptismal prayer for Helam. Following these prayers, both of them were "buried in the water."[12] After Helam's baptism, Alma baptized every other person but never again buried himself in the water.

I am particularly interested in the first prayer Alma said in the waters of Mormon, the prayer he offered for himself. Surrounded by hundreds of onlookers, alone in his newfound prophethood, Alma faithfully reached for heaven with a prayer of supplication: "O Lord," he says, "pour out thy Spirit upon thy servant, that he may do this work with holiness of heart."[13] Standing in those pure waters by that thicket of trees, Alma pled with the Lord that in spite of the humility of his singular human life, he might do the work he knew in his heart was his in a way that set his life apart for a sacred purpose—in holiness. Only after this prayer does he, with confidence, go forward and baptize the approximately four hundred fifty people waiting.

There is no question that Alma the prophet is what we would call a holy man, that the entirety of his life from the

---

12 Mosiah 18:14.
13 Mosiah 18:12.

point in which he forsook the life of a king's priest for the life of outcast prophet was holy, but how are we defining holy? We may answer that he was holy because he was a divinely appointed prophet of God. Yes, he was that, but his prophet status wasn't what made him holy. What really made him holy was that he lived his life in such a way that he set himself apart from the other priests. He did this by being humble, teachable, and willing to change his mind when Abinadi came on the scene. Remember, in the moment he chose Christ over convenience, he wasn't Alma the great prophet. He was just a young, ordinary, rank-climbing man who heard the truth and chose holiness. Throughout his life, he continued to grow in holiness, setting his life more and more apart for the purposes of heaven. His practicing holiness is not something he did because he was a prophet; his choosing holiness was what qualified him to be the prophet.

Holiness isn't a status we attain at some point. It isn't a thing. It's a practice. We can all choose to practice holiness to qualify ourselves individually for what Dr. Eva Witesman, associate professor of public service and ethics at Brigham Young University, calls "a future only God could see for [us]."[14] We do this by being humble, teachable, willing to change, and open to learning and growth.

If you were to ask me if I am a holy person, I would say, "No, I'm just a regular person trying, failing, trying again, completely unqualified in any way to claim the label of holy." However, going back to my experience in college, when I chose my integrity over my acting career, I was practicing holiness.

14 Eva Witesman. *Women and Education*, "A Future Only God Could See for You," June 27, 2017, BYU Speeches; Henry B. Eyring. "Education for Real Life," *Ensign*, October 2002.

I was choosing to set my life aside for a sacred purpose. In leaving the university, I ended up taking a stand, which led to a long and very public battle. I was misunderstood, ostracized, maligned, and mocked. My career and character in my field were decimated. What was once a booming, lucrative, and carefully built career withered and died in the lies and misconceptions.

My life became different from the one I had planned and prepared.[15] And although losing my future as a professional New York City actor was hard, it was the life I chose. I am not a victim to it. I am a chooser of the holy. In leaving the university and taking such a public stand against their discrimination, I took a step into the pure water. In seeing that I could do it, my actions inspired many people all over the world who had many different belief systems to reach into themselves and find the courage to step into their own pure water and choose holiness as they likewise stood up for their firmly held beliefs.

Holiness can be defined as Alma's decision to step out of the life of a priest and into the waters of Mormon, and I humbly suggest that my decision to stand up for my value system when I was eighteen was likewise a holy decision. Perhaps as you read this, memories of your own holy choices are brought to the surface of your mind. You too are holy. You are set apart for a sacred purpose. Even reading this book suggests that your desire is to live a life of holiness of heart.

Part of being a woman in Christ's Church is to choose a life set apart in both the big and small things. Sometimes this looks like taking a stand, and sometimes it looks like taking a nap so we have the mental fortitude to face life in a fresh and Spirit-filled

15 The happy part of this story is that many years later, I found my way back to theatre on my own terms. I perform in the community and professionally, and I teach! It isn't Broadway, but it is still full of joy.

way. It is holy to be a scholar of the gospel, and it is holy to read a book to a child and hear godliness in their little laugh. How was Alma's public stand more holy than the humble prayer for the welfare of his son? How can we suggest that the size and scope of one's work determines its significance?

> Holiness isn't a state of piety but a choice to set our life apart from what the natural woman would choose.

Alma knew his work in big and small ways, and in the times we are most honest with ourselves, we know ours. No matter our age, financial status, race, or ability, we are created in the image of deity and have the power, as Alma said, "to stand as witnesses of God at all times and in all things, and in all places that ye may be in, even until death."[16]

As women, we stand, like Alma, in the fountain of pure water that is our individual life's purpose. Our families, life callings, ambitions, worthy pursuits, dreams, hopes, talents, heartfelt desires, responsibilities, and divine foreordinations wash around our legs. Looking to heaven, we cry out with Alma's words, "O Lord, pour out thy Spirit upon thy servant [daughter] that [s]he may do this work with holiness of heart."[17] We know that the real definition of holiness isn't a state of piety but a choice to set our life apart from what the natural woman would choose, opting instead for a life of sacred purpose. This is what holy is. This is what we choose.

---

16 Mosiah 18:9.
17 Mosiah 18:12.

Chapter Two
the holiness of agency

*"Tell me, what is it you plan to do with your one
wild and precious life?"*[18]

—Mary Oliver

Here is the most liberating news: you get to choose your life.

It's an uncomfortable truth at first. Believe me, I know it is tempting to believe the lie that life is happening to us and that we are just along for the ride. After all, if life is happening *to* us, then we aren't responsible for any of it. What a relief that would be! Yet, if we aren't responsible for any of it, we don't get the credit for any of it either. If life is happening to us, we can't be proven. And isn't that the point of this whole mortal life thing? In Abraham, we read that God said, "And we will prove them herewith, to see if they will do all things whatsoever the Lord their God shall command them."[19] It was so important to God for us to choose that He was willing to give His Only Begotten Son in the

---

18 Mary Oliver. *The Summer Day, New and Selected Poems*, 1992, Beacon Press.
19 Abraham 3:25.

name of agency! He knew the plan of agency required this sacrifice. He knew He would have to withdraw His presence from His Son for a time and watch as this perfect Son suffered above all human suffering and felt abandoned and

> "Agency," I say. "I love it. I'm a huge fan!"

completely alone. God chose to allow it all in the name of agency. In a world that gives their agency away in big and minute ways every day, how "set apart" is it to be conscientious choosers? Even using our agency makes us holy.

I am a big advocate of agency. "Agency," I say. "I love it. I'm a huge fan!" But I'm afraid that sometimes (okay, I'll admit it, *sometimes* should read: MANY times) I *say* I'm a believer in agency, but I *act* like a person who believes life is happening to me. There is a word for people like this—the ones who say they love agency but then don't act like it. It's a yucky word . . . We hate being called this . . . We hate thinking of ourselves as this . . . Okay here it is . . . *victims*. (Blech! Yuck! I know! I hate that word too!) But sadly, it's true: we just love being victims. If someone else is responsible for where I am in life, I am not accountable. And that's important because being accountable can feel like the worst responsibility when the stakes are high.

Not too long ago, my tendency to distance myself from accountability was made apparent when I went running with my friend. This particular friend, Kandee, is a transplant to Utah who has brought with her such effervescence and honesty that I am absolutely positive Utah will never be the same. How I ever managed without her is a mystery to me! As we ran, I was (through labored breaths—I am most assuredly not a seasoned runner) lamenting the awful state of a situation in my life. I had decided that my life had happened to me, and I was trapped—doomed to a mediocre existence. This entrapment was, in my mind, no fault of my own. I was trapped by decisions of my youth, my husband's choices, my children, friends, family, employment, and, of course, the biggest villain of them all: the cultural expectations heaped on Latter-day Saint women. It was a piteous tale, to be sure, complete with many villains and me—me, perfectly cast as the heroic, self-sacrificing martyr. After finishing my story with a heaving breath and sigh, I awaited the inevitable outpouring of love and sympathy.

"Wow. That's a really great story you're telling yourself there," Kandee said with a sly smile. "I see why you would want to tell it to yourself that way."

Wait one second. This didn't sound like sympathy. When I looked at her in confusion, she went on to retell the story I had told her. Only, in her retelling, I was responsible for where I was in life. Those whom I had cast as villains were supporting players in a life that my choices had created. In her version, I was the villain . . . but I was also the hero.

Initially, I was resistant to her assertions. But then, as I listened, something happened. I began to feel the rope of my story that I used to bind myself with begin to loosen its suffocating grip. I began to breathe deeper. The feeling of entrapment began slipping away. In Kandee's version, I was not, in fact, trapped by anything. In her version, my choices had brought me to this exact place in my life, and my choices could get me out of any life situation. I could say no! I could become something different! I could reframe my thoughts!

In her version, the choices I made weren't entrapping; they brought me all the beauty in the very blessed life I live. In her version, everything was just right as it was but changeable if that was what I wanted. I was not a victim. I was a victor.

Isn't our most basic spiritual desire to be with God again? This requires us to choose holiness and choose God's plan. Yet, in far too many situations, we allow fear of making the wrong decision keep us stuck in a state of non-choice or self-inflicted, blind compliance. Perhaps we go about our days letting life happen *to* us, then think we have an excuse to blame others when things don't go as we'd hoped. We fail to recognize that not using our agency was, in fact, a choice.

We have to stop walking around as robots in the existence others choose for us. Sometimes we falsely call this obedience, but it is only following out of fear, not because of agency. Living life as victims was not God's plan, nor was it the plan the Savior was willing to die for. In the past, I've told myself that not choosing (being a victim) and allowing others the blame and credit for my circumstances would keep me safe, but it hasn't worked yet. Obedience to God's plan requires me to have faith in myself as I make choices, and faith in the Atonement to offer grace when my best efforts to choose fall short.

If we aren't of our own mind but are, instead, controlled by other voices, how can we stand at the judgment seat someday? Victimhood doesn't keep us safe for heaven; it takes us away from the very progression that would qualify us for heaven through use of Christ's Atonement.

We could conjecture all day long about who teaches us to be victims: society, parents, culture, religion, etc. But that would be another vain effort to lay blame. Learning to take responsibility for our lives and to choose God's plan for us is our job here on earth. It feels unstable and insecure not to know what comes next, to accept that I am the one who will have to choose my path, but it's a shaky, baby's-first-steps kind of exhilaration!

Let's not give away our agency; instead, let's learn to recognize it as one of the most sacred gifts God has given us—one of the most holy. Don't be afraid. If your heart is in the right place, you can't mess things up so badly they're beyond repair. No longer is life happening to you. Sis, you are happening to life. Victor, not victim!

During the run that day, when my friend was brave enough to be honest with me, I felt excitement about the future for the first time in a year. I can do and be whatever I want to do and be. I can, with my agency, prove myself to God! What a liberating way to think. Nothing changed that day, and yet, everything changed. My circumstances were the same, but while I had stepped onto the running trail in despair, I left it with hope and anticipation for a future that God and I got to co-create. Everyone needs a friend like my Kandee, who will kick you in the rear when you're wrong, then give you a big hug afterward.

As we seek the holy life, we must recognize that our agency is the crux on which our tests hinge. Agency is key in what we choose to do with our lives, whom we choose to associate with, what we think, how we feel, what we do with our questions, and how we progress.

It becomes difficult to seek a holy life when we allow the voices of others to drown out our own. What lies are we telling ourselves about our circumstance and situation? Who are we telling ourselves is responsible for having brought us to this moment?

Sister, you have the power to change right now. Don't be too hard on yourself for the past. You did your best; now just look forward. Tomorrow will be a better version of you. Dr. Maya Angelou says, "I did then what I knew how to do. Now that I know better, I do better."[20]

And God is waiting to help us. "Ask, and it shall be given you; seek, and ye shall find; knock, and it shall be opened unto you: for every one that asketh receiveth; and he that seeketh findeth; and to him that knocketh it shall be opened."[21]

I know intimately and heartbreakingly that discussions about agency can be unsettling, even triggering to the most wounded parts of ourselves. Without question, there are times when we are stripped of our agency.

Mental illness can preclude us from our ability to choose. Depression, anxiety, personality disorders, and other mental illnesses are very real. In his October general conference address in 2013, Elder Jeffery R. Holland jumped into the fire with his talk, "Like a Broken Vessel." Thanks to this transparent discourse, those suffering with mental illness felt, perhaps even for the first time, not quite so alone. He said, "I am speaking of . . . an affliction so severe that it significantly restricts a person's ability to function fully, a crater in the mind so deep that no one can responsibly suggest it would surely go away if those victims would just square their shoulders and think more positively— though I am a vigorous advocate of square shoulders and positive thinking!"

Additionally, seeming to strip us of our agency are the times when other people use their agency to cause permanent

20   http://www.oprah.com/oprahs-lifeclass/the-powerful-lesson-maya-angelou-taught-oprah-video.

21 Matthew 7:7–8.

> We always have the ability
> to choose the meaning
> we attach to the events
> in our lives.

changes in our lives in ways we never would have chosen. Abuse, wrongs against us, others' indifference, neglect, crimes, and carelessness are all ways we can feel stripped of our agency.

While we cannot choose everything that happens in our world, and in many situations, we can't just "choose happy," we always have the ability to choose the *meaning* we attach to the events in our lives. Dr. Viktor Frankl, who, after surviving Auschwitz concentration camp, developed a therapy called logotherapy, is one of the most well-known researchers of finding meaning in life events. The theory behind logotherapy suggested that the motivation of one's life is to find meaning in it and that we have control over the meaning of the things that happen to us. Frankl said, "Everything can be taken from a man but one thing: the last of the human freedoms—to choose one's attitude in any given set of circumstances, to choose one's own way."[22]

That is what the Savior did for us when He came to earth and fulfilled the Father's plan. Not only do we get to choose the direction of our lives, but we also get to choose what it all means.

---

22 Viktor E. Frankl. *Man's Search for Meaning* [New York: Pocket Books, 1963], 104.

There is an old tale that tells of a man who lost a horse. His neighbors said how sad it was. To this, he replied, "We'll see." His son went in search of the horse and found a group of wild horses, and he came back with five horses instead of one. The neighbors said how fortunate he was. To this, he said, "We'll see." The son was training one of the horses, fell, and broke his leg. His neighbors said how horrible it was that his son had fallen. To this, he said, "We'll see." A war broke out, and all the young men in the town were called up to war except the son whose leg was broken.

The parable of the old man and his son reminds us that the meaning of the events in our lives is ultimately our decision. And we can make the all-important decision to choose holiness each time. Carol F. McConkie confirms this: "Our mortal experiences offer us the opportunity to choose holiness."[23] We can choose a life set apart from the world—a holy, sanctified life—no matter what happens.

My newest sister-in-law, Kelsey, chose holiness, even when she never could have planned for the events in her life. Kelsey was excited to receive a call to serve a mission in the Brazil Fortaleza Mission. Off she went with her testimony and hopes for a successful eighteen months spreading the good news. After about nine months in the mission field, she felt sick . . . sick enough that she couldn't work . . . sick enough that she couldn't see. After trying to get well at a hospital in Brazil, she was sent home with what everyone thought was a staph infection that just wouldn't heal. Upon arriving home, she was immediately hospitalized with carbapenem-resistant enterobacteriaceae (CRE), also known as a superbug. For weeks, she hovered near death with a 50 percent

---

23 Carol F. McConkie. "The Beauty of Holiness," Ensign, May 2017.

chance of survival. She suffered permanent changes to her body and a complete alteration of her future.

Kelsey ultimately decided what her health meant to her life's story. She could have easily decided that she was a victim of her illness. After all, it robbed her of finishing her mission and of the dreams she had for her life. Instead, she decided to adopt the mind-set that this trial was placing her on her new path. Even though she didn't know what that was, she opened herself to the possibility that there was a path for her.

Week after week, Kelsey watched the nurses who cared for her in the hospital. She credits these nurses for the life-saving care she received and the hope she found. The example they set inspired her and lit the way ahead. Two years have passed, and my sister Kelsey is now thriving in nursing school (not the accounting program, as she had planned) and is just a few short months away from caring for patients herself. I imagine the care they will receive will be a little more tender, a little more focused, a little more holy because their nurse knows what it's like to suffer as they suffer.

Thinking of difficult life circumstances begs the questions, Did God allow these things to happen to us, or did He intentionally put them in our path? I recently spent several hours at a beautiful mountain cabin with my friend Ginger discussing, debating, and analyzing this very question. (I love philosophical friends, and Ginger is one of the best.) I can see it both ways. I could never conjure up the image of God as some all-powerful disciplinarian up in the sky, doling out life's most painful experiences: "You get cancer! You get abuse! And you get divorce!" That is not the God I know. The God I know says something like, "What is happening to you is part of the plan of agency. Because I want every person to choose, I allow these things to happen to you. I don't stop them. But I ache and mourn with you. I send the Holy Ghost to comfort you. I even provided my Only Begotten Son as a Savior for you so you would not be alone in this."

And yet . . .

If you were to ask me to list the very best things about me, I can draw a straight line back to the worst things that have happened in my life. My compassion, my dedication to my children, my advocacy, my very testimony in our loving Savior's Atonement—all these were forged in the fire of my anguish. I

> We get to choose.
> And in so choosing, we draw a little bit closer to heaven, a little bit closer to the women both we and God know we can be.

would not give one of those most horrible experiences back. They are a part of me. That is not to say that those hard things didn't break me; they did. It is certainly not to say that I would care to experience them again; I wouldn't. Additionally, there aren't words strong enough to declare with unequivocal vehemence that I do not condone hard things happening to you or to me. No, I do not! But I do *accept* that they happened to me and have, due to my agency (and, let's be honest, a good therapist) made me a better person.

Which, then, is the answer? Did God allow us to have our trials or give us our trials? I don't know. But I do know that all of these principles of agency are true. We get to choose. And in so choosing, we draw a little bit closer to heaven, a little bit closer to the women both we and God know we can be. The circumstances of our lives are just circumstances. We are the ones who decide what they mean. This choice is freedom. Freedom from the pain of others' actions. Freedom from the self-flogging of mistakes. Freedom from life's challenges. Freedom from bondage. No matter what comes our way, we can "rise up and stand with our Savior, forever true to the things we've been taught. Nothing could keep us from choosing Jesus, for we love the plan of God."[24] I think this is actually a piece of what the Atonement is: the ability to be broken and then the choice to be made into a better whole; the ability to hold our trials in a sacred space and contemplate with wonder and awe what we allowed them to help us to *become*.

Being broken is normal. Once our eyes are open to the miracle that is our own agency and we become brave enough to use it, we are going to fall. We are human. We will sin. Others will sin, and we will have to decide what to do with the consequences. We will be confused. We will use our best judgment to choose, and it will not always be the right choice. In these and every other circumstance, we will then use the Atonement to heal. This is the path of learning. From Eve to Jane Manning James to modern-day women of holiness, agency has been a key component of their life's path. The choices we make and the lives that go with those choices are ours to offer to God saying, *This is the totality of my earthly life, Father. I was brave. I used the gift of Thy Son and Thy plan to craft the most sacred life I could. It is my gesture of acceptance of my Savior's Atonement, His amazing grace.*

---

24 Shawna Bell Edwards. "Choose Him Again," Shawna Edwards Music 2016.

The plan of salvation, with all its nuances, tells me that I get to be with the people I love forever and that every pain I ever feel can, through the Atonement of Jesus Christ and my own choice, be consecrated to make me into an eventual goddess. This plan of complete compassion is the meaning I ultimately choose for everything in my life. It is the why, and the Atonement is the way. Choosing to believe the plan is a choice I get to make time and time and time again. In questions, doubts, trials, decisions, and life plans, this is the life I choose.

Learning to use our individual agency to create our own responses and our own frameworks of what it means to be alive is one of the most holy abilities we can cultivate in this life. Practicing agency both to act in our lives and to choose our responses to our circumstances is how we create lives set apart from the victim mentality of our earthly existence.

Your life as it exists right now is the sum of your choices and chosen reactions when you didn't get to choose. If you don't like it, use the Atonement and change it. Go and choose your life. Go right now! Be holy. Decide who you want to be, where you want to go, what you want to do. Decide what you believe and the best way to live to be the glorious person God designed when He made you. Have courage to live in integrity, and be true to what you know is right. And when bad things happen to you—and they will—remember, you get to decide what it all means. Allow yourself to be held in the flesh-torn hands of a loving Savior who is scarred for you.

When we own our ability to choose, the entire world opens up for us. Have you always wanted to be a painter, go back to school, start a business? What's your heart telling you to do, to be? You can decide to do the things you feel called by

God to do! I give you permission—and so did our Heavenly Parents when They were willing to give Their Son so that you and I would have an ability to choose. Exchanging an easy, lemming-like existence for the sacredness of our authenticity is holy. It isn't the easier way, but it is the holier way. Perhaps choice is the key that unlocks the door to our Godly potential. We get one shot at mortality. Let's live in a holy way as we choose the women we want to be!

In Mary Oliver's poem "The Summer Day," she asks, "Tell me, what is it you plan to do with your one wild and precious life?" I'd ask you the same. Sister, what is it you plan to do with your one wild, precious, and most holy life?

Chapter Three

your extraordinary, ordinary life: a personal ministry

"I just try to live every day . . . as if it was the full final day of my extraordinary, ordinary life."[25]

—Tim, *About Time*

Contrary to the way we sometimes live, our lives are not a series of to-do-list items. Sister, we have to wake up, to come alive to the wonder of the ordinary! We don't find a holy life in the pomp and circumstance; we find holiness in ordinary moments and in simple ministries.

Do you know how the Relief Society started? Does your mind jump to that room above the dry goods store where they held the first meeting of the Relief Society? Mine used to go there too. But that isn't where it all started. If the Relief Society was born in the dry goods store, it was conceived and gestated in the heart of one Margaret A. Cook.

Margaret Cook wanted to help those building the temple in Nauvoo. She'd noticed that many of them wore ragged clothes that were being destroyed from the rigorous labor. Though she

25 *About Time*. Richard Curtis, director, Domhnall Gleeson, actor, Working Title Films, 2013.

had no resources, she didn't just let the thought pass her by as impossible. She humbled herself and went to her employer, the very wealthy and devoted Sarah Granger Kimball, for support. Sister Kimball agreed to provide financial resources, and Sister Cook got to work, sewing. It went so well that Sister Kimball began to invite more women to her home to help. As the sewing circle grew, the women decided they wanted to form a ladies' society, which, when organized by the power of the priesthood, ultimately became the Relief Society.[26]

The Relief Society organization has always been in the plan. How could it not have been? Eliza R. Snow said, "Although the name may be of modern date, the institution is of ancient origin. We were told by our martyred prophet that the same organization existed in the church anciently."[27] Heavenly Father's desire to restore the Relief Society in the latter days came to fruition because of one ordinary woman's personal ministry. Is there anything more commonplace than sewing work shirts for a few men to wear during manual labor? And yet, she changed the world.

God did not need her to be highly educated; instead, He gave her the ability to sew. God did not need her to be rich; He gave her a wealthy and willing-to-act employer. God did not need her name to be known; she is known to Him.

He did, however, need her to be brave, bold, humble, in tune to receive revelation, ready to act upon inspiration, and willing to use the knowledge and skills she possessed to bring light and goodness to the world.

26　A more comprehensive account of Sarah Granger Kimball and Margaret A. Cook can be found in *Saints: Volume 1* (The Church of Jesus Christ of Latter-day Saints), 447–450.

27　Eliza R. Snow. Quoted in *Daughters in My Kingdom*, 7.

From the simple act of sewing shirts to the worldwide efforts of over 7 million women today, Margaret A. Cook's willingness

> She was holy—
> just as she was.

to follow through with her own personal ministry changed the trajectory of modern-day humanity. The Relief Society has given millions of women a haven of gospel learning, a tradition of offering humanitarian aid, and countless opportunities for personal development. These opportunities have enabled members to support and sustain our brothers and sisters all over the world. Next time you participate in a Relief Society meeting, perhaps your mind will turn to the poor, simple, and divinely inspired sister whose ordinary ministry paved the way for all of us to be part of something so miraculous! She sits on the pages of our history with little fanfare, but we can speak her name: Margaret A. Cook. She was holy—just as she was.

My friend Sheila Morrison runs a swimming program from her indoor pool. Her program is well respected and known in the community. If you want your child to swim quickly and effectively, Sheila's program is the most efficient I've found.

She is a bold Canadian who goes to garage sales, searches for good deals, teaches swimming lessons, always has her hands in an array of service projects, has a "little free library" in her yard, and is a mom and grandma. You might say Sheila is just a regular woman, but she is anything but ordinary. She is holy.

Every Thursday night, you'll find Sheila in her pool with her favorite students, children with disabilities. It is her favorite job. And she won't accept one penny for her services with these children. She didn't plan this ministry; it found her years ago while she was teaching swimming lessons at a community pool.

A mother came in with her son Jace[28], who had a disability. One of Jace's arms was smaller than the other and immobile, and the other arm had only partial mobility. Jace loved participating in Scouting, and his troop had an upcoming swim test that each boy had to pass to be allowed to participate in the summer's activities. Requirements for the test included jumping feet first into water over the head, leveling, swimming twenty-five feet on the surface, stopping, turning, and resuming swimming back to the starting place. Jace begged his mother for swimming lessons so he could accomplish a task his mother knew was unattainable for him. In spite of the odds, Jace's mom decided she would try to find someone who would give her son lessons, even if it was someone who would simply help Jace learn how to float more effectively in his life jacket. She knew that wouldn't be enough to pass the swim test, but as any mother would when faced with her child's dreams, she committed to try.

Jace's name and noted physical limitations were placed on a board at the pool with other children's names as a prospective student. Sheila watched as many instructors declined to teach Jace, and then one day, she took Jace's name off the board, a sign that she would be the one to teach him in spite of what everyone thought about his abilities. As everyone who knows Sheila realizes, no one tells Sheila what can and can't be done in the water!

Lesson after lesson, Sheila worked with Jace until one day, she heard the clear voice of the Spirit above the splashing in the pool.

---

28 Name has been changed.

The impression said, "Take off his life jacket." Sheila said no to the impression. Jace didn't have the ability. He could make great progress in his love for the water. He could even float around while the other Scouts were swimming, but he would never be able to pass the Scouting test. One, then two more times, the Spirit prompted. She stopped the lesson, looked into Jace's eyes, and saw his pleading. She saw the hope he had of being like his friends. She saw a human being who was capable. "Take off his jacket," she heard again. And this time, she listened.

"Well, Jace," Sheila said. "I guess we are taking off your life jacket."

She took a life vest-less Jace to a part of the pool where she could stand but he could not. She placed his feet on her legs and told him that when she said go, he was to push off of her legs and swim. Jace's mother looked on in near panic from the pool deck as her son prepared to try swimming for the first time.

"Go," Sheila said.

And that beautiful, perfect boy swam his limited mortal shell just a few feet. Sheila went the few feet, picked him out of the water, and braced her legs to have him try again. For weeks, they practiced, eventually ending up at the deep end. To everyone's amazement, Jace was ready for his test.

Sheila was prepared to be a vessel to bring goodness to Jace's life, but she doesn't give herself the credit. She says, "The Spirit didn't speak to me for my own benefit. Whether or not Jace passed his BSA swim test wasn't important to me, but it was really important to Jace. He wanted to be a full, participating member of his troop. He didn't want to be different. It wasn't my faith that took Jace's life jacket off of him that day. It was his faith. I was just the instrument through which Jace's faith was rewarded."

As Jace swam toward her for the first time, Sheila felt that she'd been given a gift in teaching and felt a personal ministry being placed upon her shoulders. Years of prior experience with children of differing abilities and her experience with Jace led her to start a program that has taught hundreds of children with disabilities to swim. Sheila has extended her love for people with disabilities by inviting other children and teenagers to be mentors to the students. It is especially redemptive for graduates of her program when Sheila invites them to return as mentors to help teach younger kids how to swim.

If you've ever wondered if swimming lessons are holy, visit Sheila's pool on a Thursday night. This holy site is extraordinarily simple: a pool full of people who love to swim. For a moment, whether or not they have a limited mind or body is inconsequential. Their differences are swallowed up in the waves and splashes of a humble backyard pool and one woman's life's work.

And Jace? The day Sheila took off his jacket was the day he left his disability at the side of the pool. When the time came for the swim test, Jace passed. And he swam with the Scouts happily ever after.

* * *

We are holy and have holy ministries. Sheila wasn't particularly comfortable with being labeled as holy, but who is? All of us ought to learn to get comfortable with this title. Our divine nature says, "I have inherited divine qualities, which

I will strive to develop."[29] We are daughters of God, created in the image of our Heavenly Mother. Our very nature leads us to perform holy, individual, divine ministries.

> Ministry looks
> like you.

What does an ordinary personal ministry look like? It looks like my neighbor Trisha bringing me lunch each week for the entire nine months I was on bed rest. It looks like Lindy, an accomplished composer of music in my stake who is constantly writing and arranging songs for simple things like girl's camp and women's conference. It looks like my across-the-street pal Xiomi who has made it her personal mission to master the art of stepmothering. It looks like Kirsten, a mom who arranged care for her own children so she could be a "Ma" (leader) to my daughter during our stake youth conference trek. It looks like my daughter picking out flowers at the market to give the sisters to whom she ministers. It looks like my friend Adrienne using her music degree to start a music class for children. It looks like my yoga guru, Julie, who runs a yoga studio and has given hundreds of people skills that help them find peace.

Ministry looks like you. I see ordinary lives every day in the women around me, and their ministry is exquisite.

Being young does not preclude you from doing great things, and being old does not exclude or excuse you. Discover your personal ministry because even a small ministry can make a huge difference.

In a recent BYC youth meeting I attended, my bishop, Bishop Atkinson, made an excellent point. He said we should

---

29 *Church Handbook of Instructions* 2:10.1.4.

not ask *what* we are supposed to do but, rather, *who* we should do things for. Let's not worry so much about what we are to do. If we stand in holy places and choose to put Christ at the center, *He* will guide us. "In all thy ways acknowledge him, and he shall direct thy paths."[30] He will make you extraordinary!

Do we look at ourselves and see only obscurity? Sis, we are not obscure. I am not obscure, you are not obscure, and the small and simple things we do each day to hasten the work of our Father in Heaven are vital to the plan. It is time for us to raise ourselves out of obscurity and own the powerful women that we are.

Each of us at times feels called to something. When we spend our days doing the things we feel called to do, be their scale large or small, life becomes rich, warm with meaning and purpose. When that feeling comes to us to pull us toward personal ministry, we all have excuses as to why we can't do whatever it is we are feeling called to do. Maybe we are too busy, too overwhelmed, don't have enough time or money. These sound like great excuses. We justify having excuses because we have an unrealistically grand view of what it means to have a personal ministry. We think ministries have to be big and elaborate. I sulked for three weeks after not being able to find the money to go help in an orphanage at the base of Mount Kilimanjaro. Three weeks of self-pity before God knocked me over the head and told me He would be perfectly satisfied if I volunteered for two hours at a shelter for those experiencing homelessness in my own area. My "I don't have the resources to serve God's children in the way I'd like" excuse

---

30 Proverbs 3:6.

was not valid. I wouldn't have been more holy in Tanzania, and I'm not less holy working at Tabatha's Way food pantry in American Fork, Utah. My offering is what matters, not the scale in which my current circumstances allow me to offer it.

Being a mother or caregiver is not an excuse. No matter what your ministry is, you can include your children or those who depend on you in small ways. By making your ministry a priority, you will teach them to value their own life's work. You will show those you care for that both you and they have goodness to offer. And to you, my sister with a houseful of tiny humans, my sister who is caring for an aging parent, or anyone who is exhausted and depleted, do not discount what appears to you to be insignificant efforts in your ministry. Remember, it is not the scale to which you heed your heart's call; it is simply that you heed it. And isn't raising our children and caring for others one of the most sacred ministries of them all?

Having a demanding career is not an excuse. Your work can become part of your ministry. (And if your career doesn't feel like a ministry, is it perhaps time for a new career? Life is too short to give our days to things that don't bring our spirits purpose.) Our careers should not be pathways away from ministering but, rather, pathways to our highest purpose. When we look at the many ways our careers serve people, when we make those whom we serve the heroes, our work becomes full of meaning, and changes from work to purpose.

Your calling is not an excuse. My young women (yes, they are mine; for the duration of my calling, those fifty powerful girls belong to me) have loved finding passion in the things I'm passionate about. They are blessed to learn from a group of eleven adult women leaders who all have different personal ministries. Likewise, I have learned about ministry from them. My young women have gone on humanitarian trips, collected clothes for women's shelters, volunteered with refugees from Nepal, learned at the feet of women in a women's shelter, painted the nails of women in our local elder care center . . . I could go on for days. For all our talk of "millennials" or "generation z-ers," these are strong, valiant, and simply good young women. Our callings don't have to take us away from our ministries; they can teach us more about them.

Being "too" of anything does not preclude or excuse us. Too young. Too old. Too fat. Too skinny. Too late. Too trapped. Too . . . There is no "too" when it comes to divinely inspired work.

The Savior says, "I am the true light that lighteth every man that cometh into the world."[31] I picture the Savior Himself pouring His light into each of us like a beautiful shining stream, each of us receiving a unique light of personal ministry according to our Heavenly Parents' plans and our own desires. The goals, aspirations, dreams, pursuits, good works, and events we give our lives to matter.

My accountant ministers to me every April. I wouldn't be able to manage my very strange career choices (a mother-writer-speaker-trainer-podcaster-actor-singer-yogi-teacher-real-estate-investor is complicated at tax time) without my accountant. I get to do what I consider to be sacred work because my accountant does sacred work.

On Christmas Eve, our heating went out. After another company gave us an astronomical bid and told us we'd have to replace our entire heating and cooling system, a brother

---

31 Doctrine and Covenants 93:2.

in our stake came right over and fixed it for a couple hundred dollars! If Chris and Sarah didn't own a heating company, our Christmas wouldn't have been as warm and Spirit-filled

> Our small drops of good works fill our wells, and we will be left with a reservoir of goodness from which generations will drink.

as it was. The heating and cooling business is holy.

This is not to imply that every moment of your life's work will fill you with joy and sunshine. Just ask a social worker who has to tell a mother that she will never be getting her children back, or a mother who has changed seventeen diapers in a day while working from home. One by one, in spite of the difficulties of our work, our small drops of good works fill our wells, and we will be left with a reservoir of goodness from which generations will drink. Sometimes it is hard and incredibly boring work to fill a well one drop at a time, but as we listen to the Spirit and our own heart's longings, then seek to do good work in the ministry we feel called to, we will see that our lives as a whole have meaning, even through the tedious and sometimes monotonous times of life.

Discover your personal ministry—even a small ministry can make a huge difference. Patriarchal blessings, journaling, prayer, classes, and learning are all excellent ways to start to discover what it is you are meant to do in this world. But don't worry too much. If you don't find your ministry, it will find you. He will place your life's work before you, and His glory is what will make your work extraordinary!

Sister Wendy Watson Nelson said to us, "Sisters, we are in mortality now because we're supposed to be here now. The doctrine is clear on this point. And among those things we are to do while we are here on this earth is to complete the mortal assignments we were given premortally and to which we agreed. The Savior said that He came to earth to do the will of His Father who sent Him. In like manner, we are here to do the will of our Father, that same Father, who sent us."[32]

How we actualize the ministry we have been called to fulfill is up to us. It might look like the women in this chapter, sewing shirts, teaching swimming lessons, working with refugees, accounting, mothering, running a business, volunteering. It might, but it doesn't have to look like any of that. This life is your canvas, your blank notebook, your ball of clay. Elder Dieter F. Uchtdorf tells us, "As you take the normal opportunities of your daily life and create something of beauty and helpfulness, you improve not only the world around you but also the world within you."[33] Your ministry. Your life. Live each day as if it were your final opportunity to add light to the world with your ordinary, extraordinary holy life.

---

32 Wendy Watson Nelson. "For Such a Time As This," BYU Women's Conference, 2007.
33 Dieter F. Uchtdorf. "Happiness, Your Heritage," *Ensign*, November 2008.

Chapter Four
the holy calling to minister

"We will implement a newer, holier approach to caring for and ministering to others. We will refer to these efforts simply as 'ministering.'"[34]

—President Russell M. Nelson

When I was twelve years old, I was the primary caregiver for my brother, age eight, while my single mother worked long hours. My brother, Robert, would definitely want me to let it be noted that he was also *my* primary caregiver during those years. He would be right. We had a small support system of extended family, but a lot of responsibility fell on the two of us as young children. I didn't get to play with friends very often and was lonely much of the time. When I turned twelve, I was excited to be in Young Women and felt very grown up. I'd sung in the ward choir since I was eight. I felt it was high time to be leaving the Primary and moving on to what I thought would be the more advanced religious studies of the youth program.

---

34 Russell M. Nelson. "Ministering," *Ensign*, May 2018.

Lisa Vermillion was the president of the Young Women. She was a young, single, beautiful, accomplished, and very busy businesswoman. Each week, outside of youth night, Lisa set aside time in her life just for me. She arranged child care for my younger brother so I could go with her to walk her dog. She told me she needed "help" walking her sweet and very pretty black lab. We'd walk our way down 10th Avenue and around the perimeter of City Creek Canyon, where it always smelled like leaves and had a view of the Utah State Capitol building in the distance. Lisa didn't talk very much as I held the leash and the dog seemed to walk me. She'd ask questions and then let me talk as long as I wanted to. My vocabulary wasn't that of a normal twelve-year-old, and whenever I'd use a large word, she'd throw her head back and laugh. She'd always look at me as if I delighted her, and we'd go on like this until the lights started turning on in the capitol building as the day gave way to dusk; that's when I knew it was time to turn around. The walks weren't long—maybe thirty minutes—but in that time, I got to feel like I was the most important person to somebody. For me, those weren't just walks. Those sacred minutes each week saved a part of me that was dying under the weight of a complicated young life. How thankful I am that Lisa was single at that time, with resources to help mother me. It's been twenty-seven years since those walks. I still know her name. I'll always know her name. And I can see her looking at me with her pixie-cut dark hair and well-defined cheeks and chin. She lives inside of me as a beautiful angel protecting my twelve-year-old heart.

Lisa would have had to walk her dog anyway, but she found a way to use an everyday chore as a tool to minister to me. No one wants to feel like a project, and walking the dog let me feel needed as she ministered. Sister Joy D. Jones rhetorically asks, "Can such a godly focus apply in everything we do? Can performing even a menial task become an opportunity to demonstrate our love and devotion to Him? I believe it can and will."[35]

For a year now, we have been immersed in the refreshing message of ministering. Every meeting, every council seems to, in some way, address the topic as we seek to quickly change our culture into something the Savior will more readily recognize as His people when He returns. Each time we discuss it, I feel like I learn something new—perhaps a fresh way of approaching how I care for others or an idea on how to minister to others as I pray. I feel myself becoming.

When the prophet says "higher and holier," we think of a better, more enlightened way, but I also think that Christ, through His prophet, is asking us to take ministering upon us, not as an "action item" to complete for a report but as a profound part of our discipleship.

As a church, we have always been good at service. It's one of our trademarks. And there will always be a need for service. Yet, ministering is deeper than service—it's more permanently committed. While service comes and goes, ministering stays. Service is focused on action-oriented offerings and finite events: bringing dinner, doing yard work, running errands. If I serve you, it is often with an in-and-out, one-and-done approach to complete a list of tasks or events. These are usually wonderful things, but when they are over, they are over. Additionally, one-sided service can make someone feel like a project. No one wants to be a checked box or a project. This strips people of their humanity.

---

35 Joy D. Jones. "For Him," *Ensign,* November 2018.

Ministry, however, is infinite. If I minister to you, I accept *you* as part of my stewardship on earth—as part of my ministry. All aspects of your welfare become paramount to me, and I strive to love and see you as the Savior loves and sees you. I become part of your eternal, epic story, and you become part of mine. I never "clock out" from you. Certainly, ministry includes acts of service, but it isn't limited to them. Ministry seeks to give from a complete knowledge of another's unchangeable worth and value. At a community luncheon I attended recently, social scientist Arthur Brooks said, "If we truly want to help others, we have to need them." Ministry gives people their humanity as it loves from a place of equal need.

How we minister will be taught to us, and we will be given the bravery needed to minister when we remember *who* we are really ministering for. Sister Joy D. Jones says, "We [are] doing it for Him. He made the struggle no longer a struggle."[36] The Savior is asking for our help in caring for those He loves. Sometimes I think about our Heavenly Family and sit in awe of Their plan. They love us infinitely, but They didn't want to compel us to choose Them, as was suggested by another brother, so They allowed Christ to atone for us in the hopes that we would use our agency to choose Father's plan and come back to Them. Then They allowed us to come to earth. They see all that we suffer, from the tiniest setbacks to the biggest heartbreaks. They want to comfort us and can from Their lofty estate in many ways. Yet, They know there are ways to help us that They cannot accomplish without another person. They know we have the potential to help each other find our way back to Them. They long for us. That's where all of us come in. (Big side note: There are times when I'm writing that I feel like a fraud. Usually,

---

36 Ibid.

it's when I start trying to tell you what or how to do something. This is no exception. I feel like a bossy sister. I started writing about how to

> **There is nothing as transcendently divine as having loved someone else with the pure love of Christ.**

pray for those you minister to and then added to the list of action items. It felt wrong. Because it isn't about that, is it, sis? As far as your ministry goes, I can't tell you what to do or how to do it. I really do want to give you some great checklist, but I can't. You'll have to go to the Source and ask, as He, the One who died for them, is the One who knows how you are supposed to minister to your sisters.)

Sister Joy D. Jones shared how she and her husband were guided to minister. She says, "As we sought direction from the scriptures, the Lord taught us how to make the process of serving others easier and more meaningful."[37] The Lord Himself, through His scriptures and the Spirit, will teach each of us how to minister as we earnestly seek to know.

While I don't know a lot about your whos, whats, whens, or hows of ministering, I do feel I can testify to the why. Why do we do it? Why do I do it? I feel the most like the person I really am and the godly woman I can eventually become when I listen to the Spirit's call on behalf of other people, then move forward with imperfect action. There is nothing as transcendently divine as having loved someone else with the pure love of Christ. It's a feeling unlike any other that combines the natural rush of

---

37 Ibid.

dopamine, a sense of satisfaction, and the gratitude of having been used for a sacred purpose into a burst of light so pure and holy that it feels like what I imagine heaven will feel like. It reminds me who I'm living for—my Savior! I've come to crave this feeling. This is the why.

This higher and holier change to ministering isn't about making things easier or managing the logistical side of the Church of Jesus Christ. In fact, the change has probably made that side of things a lot harder. It's about changing our hearts from the inside out. Unless we embrace this shift in how we care for one another, we won't see what's possible in our communities. President Jeffrey R. Holland offers this: "I warn you, a new name, new flexibility, and fewer reports won't make an ounce of difference in our service unless we see this as an invitation to care for one another in a bold, new, holier way."[38]

It's good to be assigned to minister to someone, but we shouldn't feel as if the scope of our ministry is limited to an official Church-issued assignment. "And if it so be that you should labor all your days in crying repentance unto this people, and bring, save it be one soul unto me, how great shall be your joy with him in the kingdom of my Father! And now, if your joy will be great with one soul that you have brought unto me into the kingdom of my Father, how great will be your joy if you should bring many souls unto me!"[39] We don't have to, and actually shouldn't, wait for an assignment to minister to others. This is a higher and holier way.

Within each of our hearts is a pull to minister, not only to those to whom we are assigned but also to the world. My friends

38 Jeffrey R. Holland. "Be with and Strengthen Them," *Ensign,* May 2018.
39 Doctrine and Covenants 18:15.

Sandi and Mike run a food pantry called Tabitha's Way for the hungry in our community and also support a training school for incarcerated individuals to transition to the workforce. My brother, Robert, volunteers with survivors of abuse and is a key player in the fight against the opioid epidemic in the state of Utah. Lisa, my dear friend, is a teacher and member of the PTA, the Primary president, and a child advocate. My sister-in-law Amber has served for years on district and school community councils. My friend Holly went on five humanitarian trips last year. My sister Erin takes sodas and cookies to the secretaries at her kids' school. My friend Helen travels all over the world, bringing dolls to refugee camps. Debbie, my sweet friend, is the quintessential neighborhood mom who is happy to shuttle, support, and encourage her own kids, mine, and many others as well. I know these can sound like big things. You might be tempted to think I just know a lot of "movers and shakers," but the truth of the matter is, these amazing people are just my friends and neighbors in my middle-class life who are just living their own normal lives. When their ministries have called, they have found ways to magnify them. Each one of us is amazing and has unlimited potential. My friends are from all different socioeconomic backgrounds. Some are young; some are older. None of their circumstances has stopped them! And you . . . you do extraordinary things too; perhaps none more important than listening to a friend or holding a baby in the grocery line so his mom can pay for her groceries hands-free. I could write for pages about every person in my life and the ways they serve Christ by loving those for whom He died. Each of these people has taken upon them a holy and sacred ministry. They are doing it every day. Imperfectly, by the way. Your ministry and those who are depending on you within that ministry are calling to you.

Elder Uchtdorf reminds us to "consider the act of seeking out the poor and the needy, lifting the hands that hang down, or blessing the sick and afflicted. Aren't these the very acts of pure ministering the Lord practiced when He walked the earth?"[40]

> Just as Christ knew how to succor us because He bore our pain, we too will know how to comfort others who suffer as we have suffered.

I know what's happening right now. Here's the part of the chapter where you might want to say you don't know who you are supposed to minister to and you start freaking out that you don't have a holy ministry, that you don't know who you are supposed to care for because you aren't good enough and you can barely do what you are already doing, so what's the point of even worrying about knowing what your ministry is anyway? Sister, stop. You know what your ministry is and who it's for. It's the thing that wakes you up in the night or the people who fill you with concern. It's where you love to spend your time and feel fulfilled when you leave. Look to the things that bring you joy. Look to your past pain that is now healed through the Atonement of Jesus Christ as an invitation to your ministry. Just as Christ knew how to succor us because He bore our pain, we too will know how to comfort others who suffer as we have suffered. And through our love, we will show them the way home.

---

40 Dieter F. Uchtdorf. "Believe, Love, Do," *Ensign,* November 2018.

Better? Okay. Now find your quiet calm. Breathe in. Breathe out. There. Do you hear it? The answer is inside you. So be brave, and "Go, and do thou likewise."[41]

I don't think it matters where we go to minister, only that we go. In Paul's epistle to the Colossians, he told the Saints, "Take heed to the ministry which thou hast received in the Lord, that thou fulfill it."[42] Today's ministering doesn't wait for an invitation; it goes and does in the direction of the heart's pull.

My new friend Chase Hansen and his dad, John, taught me what this means. I met Chase (age nine) at a bipartisan solutions summit focusing on the opioid epidemic. One of the breakout sessions was for members of the community to better understand how they could help. The room felt sacred to me. There is a sacred feel to rooms full of people with honest hearts and many different ways of thinking, people who are willing to put their differences aside for a common good.

It was a room full of government officials, business executives, faith leaders from many denominations, and community members. We were all united in spirit to take an honest look at a crisis in our community and brainstorm ways we could help. Among the big thinkers sat a little boy, listening intently and occasionally whispering to his dad. I would come to see that he was perhaps the biggest thinker of us all. As one of the panelists sought to illustrate a point he was making, he asked Chase to stand and explained that Chase was a leader in the community and ran Project Empathy, a nonprofit with the goal of eradicating homelessness one human connection at a time.

---

41 Luke 10:37.
42 Colossians 4:17.

I got more of Chase's story after the session when I ran into him and his dad in the hall. Chase passionately told me about his project and about all he was learning and doing for the community. He let me ask him questions.

"Who is this kid?" I thought.

Project Empathy started when Chase was four years old and he and his dad, dressed like superheroes, walked to a comic convention. Chase asked about the people sleeping on the ground. His dad explained that they were people experiencing homelessness.

"What's homelessness?" young Chase wondered.

"It's when people don't have a home."

"Why don't they have homes?" Chase asked. And all the "why" questions of a four-year-old came spilling out.

John's response to the questions of his son was, "I don't know, Chase, but let's find out together."

And they have. Over the course of five years, from that day to now, Chase and his dad have done many things to help the homeless, all at Chase's lead. They've founded a resource center, raised money for mattresses for the homeless shelter, volunteered with various groups, and conducted a wealth of social experiments in the community. Yet the most powerful thing I believe they've done with Project Empathy is also their favorite. Weekly, they meet with one person experiencing homelessness to share a meal and exchange stories. It isn't about the food; it's about the connection.

"We have to eat anyway," Chase told me. "We might as well eat together and learn about each other's lives. When I ask the people what they need, they usually say they need to talk about their stories. They are just like us. They just want love and for someone to notice them."

In the five years since Project Empathy began, Chase and John have been recognized by government and religious leaders for their work, have had a meal with over one hundred thirty people experiencing homelessness, and have developed continuing friendships.

John and Chase didn't wait to be invited to help those experiencing homelessness; they just went to work ministering. What changes their offering into ministering rather than service is their conviction, love, commitment, and belief that the people experiencing homelessness have something to offer. When Chase and John sit down to a meal with one of their new friends, they are careful to offer the meal in exchange for the new friend's companionship. They make their new friends feel needed and equal as they spend a few moments of their day breaking bread together.

Chase and John don't see themselves as being above ministering to those "below." They truly see the people with whom they share lunch as friends with as much to offer as anyone else. "Bias and judgment come from a place other than fact," John says. The real fact is that each individual is of infinite worth to God, and love is the quickest way to gain a testimony of that. Elder Uchtdorf said, "Through the lens of pure love, we see immortal beings of infinite potential and worth and beloved sons and daughters of Almighty God. Once we see through that lens, we cannot discount, disregard, or discriminate against anyone."[43]

People are ministered to when they know they're connected, that they are the same, and that they are important. I was particularly touched to hear John say he is not a member of The Church of Jesus Christ of Latter-day Saints but that his son is and Project Empathy is part of Chase's ministering effort!

43 Dieter F. Uchtdorf. "Believe, Love, Do," *Ensign,* November 2018.

Here is a father, not of our faith, supporting his son's responsibility to minister. It's beautiful. John notes that as a parent, it is important to create op-

> "Plant the word in your hearts, that ye may try the experiment of its goodness."

portunities for our children to minister through one-on-one, person-to-person connections. He sees himself simply as a facilitator of Chase's ministry.

As the Church moves to a home-centered, Church-supported model for our worship, it becomes essential that in addition to formal gospel teaching, we, like John did for Chase, help our families discover their own ministering capabilities and then provide opportunities for them to succeed in these holy callings. People learn best not just by reading and hearing lessons but also by going and doing. Alma 34:4 gives us the formula for at-home learning: "Yea, even that ye would have so much faith as even to plant the word in your hearts, that ye may try the experiment of its goodness." It is the scriptural learning that "plants the word." Once planted, it is up to us to go out into the world and "experiment of its goodness" by ministering to others and spreading the good news.

Our efforts to support our children don't have to be big like Project Empathy. With our heartfelt intentions to create an environment where our children can find ways to minister, even our small acts and words of encouragement can nurture them as they, like us, find their way to those who are waiting for them.

In January 2018, three months before the Church as a whole adopted the ministering approach to love each other, members of the Relief Society unknowingly began the shift in action and thought by adapting the way they visit taught. Instead of a correlated message, we as Relief Society members were to seek out inspiration on how to love, teach, and connect with our sisters. It was exciting to see things changing, but many of us were used to the old method and didn't know exactly how to approach this new challenge. However, my visiting teacher didn't hesitate to jump in. I got the most refreshing text that January. It said, "What kind of a visiting teacher do you need/want? Drop off a thought and treat? Sit and visit? Take you to lunch? A mix of everything?"

I loved the text, and my eyes filled with unexpected tears. She asked me directly what I needed and wanted. Though I have always had amazing visiting teachers, I don't think anyone ever asked me directly what I needed in a visiting teacher before this point. I knew exactly what I needed/wanted from her, but it felt scary, so I typed out a hasty reply, "Oh, whatever. I'm up for anything." Luckily, before I hit send, a little voice came up from my heart to my head to remind me that I did need something . . . a friend. I'd been feeling lonely and isolated, especially in a demanding calling in which we both served. Heavenly Father was trying to answer my prayer to find a friend. I found my brave and typed, "I love that you asked. Honestly, I need a friend. I don't want to feel like a check mark. I would love natural, gospel/spiritual conversations rather than an official message. I would love to go on walks, chat, go to lunch, hang out, go to the temple, etc. I need to add to my list of REAL friends." Thus began a treasured friendship that will be dear to me forever.

When those who are assigned to us—or who just want to or feel inspired to minister to us—are brave enough to act on their promptings—even if it's imperfect action—it is our responsibility to be humble enough to receive their offerings. When we're ministering, it's important to just jump in with action rather than offer the traditional "Let me know if there's anything I can do." Ofttimes our ministering sisters and brothers, through their stewardship's promptings, can anticipate what we need before we do. However, we do need to accept that we have a responsibility in the equation. It is our job to be vulnerable and allow God to answer our prayers through other people. We can't expect people to know our needs if we aren't willing to be honest, open, and forthcoming about the ways we know they can best serve us. If we know how our ministering sisters and brothers can help us, we are accountable to let them know. They aren't mind readers, and we all know from being in that position ourselves that a little guidance is always welcome. We help our ministering sisters and brothers become more adept at listening to the Spirit when we validate their promptings and allow them to serve us. Wouldn't you be thrilled if a sister you minister to shared a need she has and allowed you to fill that need for

> It is our job to be vulnerable and allow God to answer our prayers through other people.

her? Wouldn't it help you to know her and understand her better? Wouldn't it help you to understand the Spirit's whisperings on her behalf in a more effective way? Recently, a neighbor approached my husband and wondered if he would come rototill her yard. "You have that great rototiller," she said (at which we all laughed, as our rototiller came from my husband's grandparents and is probably forty years old. It's kind of a neighborhood joke, but we are so thankful to have it.) "And I," she said, "have great bread-making skills in return." They set up a time to till her yard, and when she left, my husband turned to me and said, "I'm so thankful she let me know how I could help her family." We need to teach each other how to minister to each other. It is going to require humility on both sides and faith that because of our willingness, God is working through us.

Every day, we are learning, and every day we are getting better at learning how to minister and be ministered to. One year down; eternity to go. Jesus said, "But rise, and stand upon thy feet: for I have appeared unto thee for this purpose, to make thee a minister and a witness both of these things which thou hast seen . . . To open their eyes, and to turn them from darkness to light, and from the power of Satan unto God, that they may receive forgiveness of sins, and inheritance among them which are sanctified by faith that is in me."[44] It is time for us to rise. To stand upon our feet. To minister and to be a witness of the light of God that we have seen, by loving others the way Christ would love.

This is my prayer. This is my testimony. This is one of the things I know for sure: God will give us everything we need to evolve to higher and holier ministries of love when we stand on

---

44 Acts 26:16–18.

our own two feet and move forward one imperfectly perfect step at a time. As we do so, our lives will be full of meaning, joy, and light beyond anything we understand or even deserve. In these holy moments, we can take the opportunity to look up at the sky and whisper under our breath, "I stand all amazed."

Chapter Five
taking time and finding quiet

"Take time to be holy, the world rushes on; Spend much time in secret, with Jesus alone. By looking to Jesus, like Him thou shalt be; Thy friends in thy conduct His likeness shall see."

—"Take Time to Be Holy," William D. Longstaff, 1882

I spent some time in my writing career interviewing artists, most of whom were painters, and writing about their processes. I loved it, listening to artists talk about what their work meant to them, about color, about light. There were so many life lessons I took away with me. Through the interviews, a common theme emerged that isn't as obvious to those of us whose magnum opus of visual arts is a poorly drawn cartoon from art class in the seventh grade. The artists I interviewed all talked about the importance of negative space in their work. Negative space, they taught me, is all the space around the object of focus, many times occupying more space than the design itself. Over the course of several interviews, I learned that this negative space is the most important part of a painting.

An amateur artist tries to fill in the negative space with other objects, which ends up detracting from the composition and message of the painting as a whole. An adept artist values the negative space as essential to communicating the vision of their product. Each artist I interviewed over the course of those years talked to me about the ways they use the negative space in their own personal work. It was the negative space that ended up creating pieces that were not only visually stunning but were also emotionally impactful. You'll know when you see a piece of artwork that does this well. It will take your breath away and bring emotions to the surface that leave you not wanting to look away. What is the composition of our lives? Have we left any room around our life's composition, or have we filled every bit of negative space with distractions? Holiness is born in the negative space.

When I was twenty years old, I experienced a season of choosing pathways in my young life. At an unexpected crossroads in my education and seriously dating my future husband, I found myself full of confusion. I went to my future husband's grandfather to receive a priesthood blessing. I had hope that Heavenly Father would tell me through this patriarch emeritus with kind eyes and a joking disposition that I was destined to marry his grandson . . . or not. For weeks, I'd waited for the heavens to open and angelic messengers to come down, tap me on the shoulder, and say regarding my decision to marry, "The answer is yes," but it hadn't happened. (Remember that my twenty-year-old brain wasn't fully developed. Neither was my appreciation for the Christ-sacrificing concept of agency, apparently.) I figured a blessing was the next best thing to heavenly intercession.

It was my expectation to leave that day with a clear path regarding the questions I had in my mind, but instead, I left still feeling confused about the future, though I would see the impact of the priceless divine guidance I received more clearly in the years to come. The blessing didn't address my relationship. Instead, with power, it spoke of quiet.

It was early 2000, a time when cell phones were used only to call people and were available only to the few. The internet's popularity was in its infancy. I had an email account I checked once a week. To me, the world was difficult to navigate, but it wasn't remarkably loud. In the blessing, I was informed of a forthcoming time of great noise that would come into the world and into my life. At times when I needed to rely on the Lord, I was told repeatedly to actively seek out quiet.

The blessing went on to enumerate the many ways my soul would find inspiration in the places of quiet. The specific promises are for God, Grandpa, and me alone to know, but it is enough to say that I was promised sacred blessings if I would seek quiet places. But the blessings found in quiet are not just meant for me. These blessings of direct communication with the Lord are available to everyone willing to seek them.

In the musical *Matilda*, there is a song that depicts the heroine, a little girl, in the midst of a noise-filled life of chaos. She sings about feeling the noise of the world all around her as loud raging that fills her with deep emotions, but in finding quiet, she finds an eye of the storm that offers her stillness and makes her think of lovely things.[45]

Our lives can seem like little Matilda's, immersed in uncontrollable noise. We are bombarded with metaphorical and

---

45 "Quiet," *Matilda,* the Musical. Book by Dennis Kelly, with music and lyrics by Tim Minchin.

> To seek the holy life, we have to seek the silence.

literal noise. In the midst of all this external calamity, even our thoughts become loud and full of fear. The noise and the fear build and build and build as we search for what Matilda calls "the eye of the storm," a place of quiet and warmth.

What's even more disturbing than the volume of noise we are experiencing is its dissonance. We are making noise that isn't harmonizing with our fellow humans. We're off key. Ours is a cacophonous symphony of war, contention, politics, and media. We don't even know how to make our noises work together. I picture Satan whispering to his minions, influencing the world to shout at us while he whispers the noise of lies to our hearts. If I were Satan, I too would fill the world with noise.

How can we hear our own souls anymore? Recent scientific findings suggest that our physical cells contain the DNA of our ancestors' experiences. Would not our spirits then contain the material of God? And wouldn't that spiritual DNA tell us what we need to know? What if we were quiet and could remember truth that we've always known . . . and what if that remembering could bring peace to our souls and give us strength to walk out of the eye of the storm and back into the world? Without seeking a space of silence, how can we hear our own spirit's voice? How can we hear *the* Spirit's voice?

To seek a holy life, we have to seek the silence. In the spring of 1820, Joseph didn't pray at home in the midst of the maple-sugaring work and early spring chores most likely taking place on the farm outside of the maple grove that would eventually be known as sacred. He didn't pray in his room. He didn't pray in a church. Instead, he sought for a place of quiet solitude to ask of God. It wasn't peace that Joseph immediately found while praying. Before the revelatory vision, before the light, before the peace came the dark. Of this experience, Joseph said, "I was seized upon by some power which entirely overcame me, and had such an astonishing influence over me as to bind my tongue so that I could not speak. Thick darkness gathered around me, and it seemed to me for a time as if I were doomed to sudden destruction."[46] From our own experiences with darkness and fear, we can imagine what this young boy felt as he sought divine communion and found, instead, this opposition.

Is fear what keeps us from the quiet?

The noise of the world is robbing us of our connection to the divine. And we've become so used to the incessant sound coming from everywhere that we aren't comfortable in the silence. Even when we find an unexpected moment of silence, we fill it up. If I'm driving, I'll turn on the radio. Many people even have noisemakers to put them to sleep. The world has become a place in which silence is the exception and places of actual silence are rare. But to live a holy life, we have to be able to hear the Spirit. Of course the Spirit is strong enough to find us and speak to us in the loud and the noise, but His whisperings are harder to hear with noise all around.

Sometimes we might not seek quiet because we are afraid of the layers we have to unearth to get to the quiet place. First is the layer of audible noise around us, things like the radio, television, podcasts, a noisy room, etc. Turning these

---

46 Joseph Smith—History 1:15.

off might require some intention on our part, but it is usually straightforward. Once we get through the world's noise, the remaining noise gets a little more difficult to silence: these are the layers of intangible, internal noise.

There is a layer chattering about all the to-dos, all the things we should be doing instead of being quiet: pay the bills, do the jobs, fill the time with other things. If we are strong enough to get through this layer, we find the most destructively noisy layer of them all. This is the layer of lies made up of messages of opposition from voices that aren't of God. Voices that tell us lies about not being good enough, pretty enough, worthy enough. Sometimes these noises and the fears they bring with them are enough to nearly suffocate us.

As it was with Joseph Smith, our intense search for silence amid the layers of noise might leave us feeling as if we are about to be snuffed out. But if with strength and patience we can tear through these layers, we will find a sweet place of light, peace, and understanding. This is where it is still. This is where your soul and the Holy Spirit speak to you. Revelation and inspiration live here.

Once you experience the inspiration and, dare I say, revelation found when you seek quiet, it will no longer feel like a luxury to you. It will feel like an absolutely essential element of your life, and you'll find yourself making time for it more and more often. People might judge you for seeking quiet. No, people *will* judge you. "How dare you take time and quiet for yourself when there is so much to be done?" When this happens, don't be too hard on them for their judgment. Remember, you were once a person who didn't know the value of time and quiet. And, by all means, do not allow them to make you question yourself. That self-doubt is part of the noise. When others see you hearing their feedback and choosing quiet anyway, they will pay attention. Your example might even inspire them to take time and choose quiet for themselves.

> I want to taste the sweetness of the holy life today.

What is happening in your life right now? For me, this is a season of expansion of my soul. I don't want to wait for someday to find holiness. I want to taste the sweetness of the holy life today. Don't you? President Eyring says, "This day is a precious gift of God. The thought 'Someday I will' can be a thief of the opportunities of time and the blessings of eternity."[47] We cannot wait to taste holiness sometime in the future, sister! What if everything we need is found in the time we take for quiet today?

Satan makes what I call "noise traps." Things to distract us from seeking and finding the quiet. Social media is perhaps one of the noisiest of all these traps. We are letting social media steal our quiet and our holy, sacred moments with our families, and we have to stop.

A few months ago, I noticed that my friend Abi wasn't online very much anymore. She told me she'd installed an app on her phone and was shocked to learn she was unknowingly spending many hours a day on social media all while having a job and being a mother of four busy children. She didn't know how she was possibly doing it, but the evidence was there. She

---

47 Henry B. Eyring. "This Day," *Ensign*, May 2007.

then set guidelines for herself so she could be more present with her family, the Spirit, and herself. It is working for her, and I love seeing the change in her. I want to be like her!

After listening to the prophet speak to the youth at the face-to-face event in June 2018, I, too, fasted from social media. My family had already planned a month-long fast, so with the prophet's invitation, we stuck to our plan and moved forward. My findings after being offline for so long . . . It's going to sound a little harsh: no one cares. It's true! The few, and I'm talking *few*, people who noticed my virtual absence called me to say hello. Yes, they called. On the phone. As in, we spoke with our voices to each other.

At first, the fast was hard. I found myself wanting to share the super-epic things happening in my world. (Yes, my life is super epic. Yours is too. I go to magical, envy-worthy places of adventure . . . like the exotic land of Idaho.) Mostly, I love to share my words and the things I learn so I can engage in meaningful discussion with my friends. When framed like that, my social media usage is pretty holy, right? A few times that month, I almost gave in and shared things online, but I held true. Day after day passed, and so did the urge to share. One afternoon, I was sitting at the base of a waterfall near a large swimming hole where my kids were splashing as they tried to use their hands to scoop up tadpoles. It was a sweet, charming, share-worthy afternoon, yet I sat in the sun and found great joy knowing that this sacred moment belonged only to me, my husband, and my kids. And I took pictures on my phone and wrote about it in my journal so I would never lose the moments. After a month of being electronics-free, the urge to hoard every moment of my life electronically has never come back in the same way.

Before you go thinking that I am calling social media evil, I am not. I love it. (HMU on insta y'all. Like that? The young women taught me that one. It means "hit me up," as in, "Would you please contact me?") I love connecting with my friends and sharing my life, just not at the expense of my holiness. Not anymore. So don't stop. Share away, my friends—it's so much fun—but every once in a while, when the heavens themselves seem to gift you a moment of pure beauty, consider holding on to it only for you. That is an experience set apart from the world. That is holiness.

Social media obviously isn't the only noise trap. Other seemingly great things can also try to fill our world with noise. Community commitments, extra projects at work, taking on more than you can handle, saying yes to too many things, even our callings can be thieves of our sacred time and quiet.

To stop some of the time and quiet thievery, let me give you a little tip about callings. If you want to know your job requirements and the tasks you committed to accomplish when you accepted your calling, read the Church's *Handbook 2* and ask God. No one else's opinion matters. And if a task or commitment isn't in the handbook, you didn't accept the call to do it! If the Spirit asks you to do something additional, do it. If anyone else asks you to add to your already heavy load, commit only to consider their request and then, with prayer, decide for yourself. You did not commit to make homemade doilies for the Relief Society weeknight meeting. (You may have *volunteered* to do it, but, sister, that wasn't required for your calling—that one's on you.)

Saying no can be an uncomfortable but essential inter-personal skill to develop. If you're worried about having the ability to discern when enough is enough for demands on your time, relax. You'll know what's too much for you. We have a sixth sense about these things (we just like to ignore it a lot of the time). If you feel uneasy about saying yes to something you are being asked to do, or if you start hearing that noisy dissonant sound start creeping up from your heart, be brave. With love and compassion to those demanding too much, say no. "No, I won't go to that extra meeting. I do love you though and thank you for giving me an opportunity to choose. I, too, will respect your boundaries when you need me to."

Remember, when people ask too much of you, it is most likely that they feel too much is being asked of them. The process of your saying no to something is the perfect time to practice love and compassion. This isn't an excuse not to help people or to stop going the extra mile. When you learn to say no instead of yes out of obligation, it frees you to learn how to say yes from a place of choice and agency. In this kind of yes, you'll find sacredness in your offering. The gift of your time when compelled or manipulated is self-betraying. The gift of your time offered freely from your choice is holy.

Our callings at Church, our work, our civic responsibilities—each aspect of our lives is demanding to be seen. Many of us think we have to do it all at once. In his nationally best-selling book, author (and Latter-day Saint bishop) Greg McKeown points out, "The word priority came into the English language in the 1400s. It was singular. It meant the very first or prior thing. It stayed singular for the next five hundred years. Only in the 1900s did we pluralize the term and start talking about priorities."[48] How will we find the negative space in which the Spirit speaks if we

48 Greg McKeown. *Essentialism: The Disciplined Pursuit of Less* (2014), Crown Business.

are seeking to do the impossible and focus on so many priorities? Logically, only one thing can be front and center at a time.

> Making room in our lives to experience divine personal revelation has to be our single most important task.

Equally entrapping are the cultural messages of the western world that value busyness and noise as evidence of hard work and efficacy. Those who would seek the space and time to find holiness are labeled as "lazy" or "indulgent." Holy moments of quiet are as essential to our spiritual bodies as eating is to our physical ones. You might live without, but not for long. Noise is the parasitic robber that treats us as its host and feeds from our peace, leaving us soul-starved. Making room in our lives to experience divine personal revelation has to be our single most important task. It has to be our priority. Sister Julie B. Beck said it this way: "The ability to qualify for, receive, and act on personal revelation is the single most important skill that can be acquired in this life."[49] When you are brave enough to silence the external voices and make your own time for quiet, you are exhibiting bravery and wisdom, not laziness.

Break through the noise traps! In quiet is born inspiration that will lead you to a place where you can bring your light to the world. Quiet will make a space for you to hear where God

---

49 Julie B. Beck. "And upon the Handmaids in Those Days Will I Pour Out My Spirit," *Ensign*, May 2010.

wants you to go and what you are to do. Others' lives will be bettered by the messages God will whisper to you—messages inspiring you to act on behalf of someone else. You will leave your place of quiet shining, ready to fill the world with light. "Let your light so shine before men, that they may see your good works, and glorify your Father which is in Heaven."[50]

Your example will motivate others to find courage within themselves to take time to seek this peace. You can be an advocate for time and quiet! Suggest that your employer provide meditation time at work, remove your family from the noise, teach your children to appreciate quiet, take a moment at the end or beginning of a lesson discussion you facilitate to offer a few minutes of total silence. The most helpful thing we can do for others is allow them to have their quiet. We can stop becoming part of the noise traps for the people around us and choose to be a crutch as they seek holy quiet on their own. We can do this by respecting others' boundaries. Maybe organize group hikes for your friends to be in nature. Perhaps, instead of engaging a teenager in conflict, ask if you can walk around the block in total silence together first. Or create a quiet space in your home where electronics aren't allowed. The exact right way to create quiet for you and your family will come to you just when you need it most.

Last year, I overscheduled the school year for all three of my kids and me. School started in late August, and by November, I was losing my sanity. I wanted to run away. Fast. I longed for quiet for all of us. By December 1, I had decided we were going to Vermont the following summer for one month. Why Vermont, you ask? Mostly because I knew nothing about it

50   Matthew 5:16.

and wouldn't be tempted to sightsee. I dreamed of a place of quiet, open space, of writing this book, of finding God and catching tadpoles in the summer sun. I got through a lot of four-hour carpool days that school year by dreaming of those tadpoles.

In my fantasy, we would have no contact with our world at home and no electronics. I had an obscenely low budget for this adventure. Yet I believed that if I looked hard and long enough, I could make it happen. Somehow, I found the perfect place: a little cabin next to a stream, one mile from the most perfect swimming lake and two miles from an entrance where we could hike the Appalachian Trail—a bucket-list item for me. Its already low nightly rate would be discounted if we stayed longer than two weeks. (It cost less to go to Vermont for a month than it did to take my kids to Disneyland for two park days and five total vacation days at a discount hotel! I am serious.) I booked the cabin and bought a AAA membership. We were hitting the open road. Three kids, a mom, and an eleven-year-old Dodge Durango. (And for part of the time, a husband who was able to sneak away from work for two of the four weeks of our trip.) Everyone thought I was crazy. (Not that I can blame them. My car did start to make a death-rattle noise somewhere in Chicago, and it still hasn't gone away to this day.)

Just as I had predicted, the first couple of days without electronics were hard for the kids, and let's face it, equally hard for me. Yet, after a bit, we all settled in. The kids had each other as playmates and the pen and paper journals I had given them as media. About a week into our trip, my daughter, Hailey, said, "Mom, I know this is going to sound funny, but I can *hear* myself here. My own voice. I hear it! It's like I know myself better in the quiet. Isn't that weird?" No, my gorgeous girl who is turning too quickly into a woman, it is not weird. We found in Vermont exactly what I wanted to find—a quiet nothingness to hear ourselves. To hear our God. And yes, we found, held, and delighted in tadpoles.

In complete transparency, it was a lot of planning and work. The quiet I had hoped for was definitely there, but more for my kids than for me. Somehow, if you can believe it, there were still dirty dishes and laundry in Vermont. We also had a very unfortunate rodent infestation in our cabin. Some big-deal life things were collapsing at home. And reentry into the real world when the trip was over was hard . . . like a crash-landing-in-a-fiery-explosion kind of hard. But our time there was set apart from the world for a sacred purpose. It was so very holy. I could write an entire book about the lessons we learned and the memories we made in the quiet green hills of Vermont. Maybe someday I will.

I think back on the blessing from my husband's grandfather so many years ago that told me to seek quiet. I think about the girl I was when I received that blessing. I wonder at all she had to go through from then to now and am grateful that through it all, I had the memory of that blessing from which to gain comfort. What my husband's grandpa, who would become one of the most priceless people in my life, the grandfather of my heart, didn't know the day he offered me heavenly instruction was that through his words, Heavenly Father was handing me a map to the eye of the storm. He was telling me where I would find Him and where I would find myself.

* * *

It would be beneficial for each of us to have some tools in our pockets that will help us find quiet and negative space in the artwork that is our lives. Your list may be very different from mine—no two pieces of artwork are the same. But just in case you, like me, love to hear what's working for your friends, here are some of my favorite tools:

- Vacations. Simple vacations without a lot of plans, away from the noise of the world, really help me—and my family—draw closer to Christ. The upside to these trips is that they are usually inexpensive. I gave my Vermont cabin trip as an example of this. Likewise, we have had equally transcendent experiences camping for free in the mountains or in our own backyard.

- Gardening. There is something about gardening that draws me closer to God. Turning soil with my bare hands is meditative and calming.

- Walks. Nightly walks calm me at the end of the day. My husband and I have our set route. The sound of each step on these nightly walks helps me put things in perspective and feel the Spirit.

- Singing or listening to music. It seems counterintuitive to include music as a method to achieving quiet. For literal quiet, it perhaps isn't the most effective tool. For quiet of the soul, however, there is nothing more effective. I love to sing and hear music. I have a playlist on my phone of songs I know will take me to a place of stillness within myself. In times of loudness of my heart, humming or singing can soften me.

- Controlled breathing. When I want to find peace quickly, I practice what yogis call pranayama and what the rest of us call breathing exercises. Meditation (discussed in more detail in the holy habits chapter) is essential for quieting the loud layers of my mind.

For those beginning to be brave enough to take time to be holy and find quiet, I thought it might be helpful to include a list of places in my life that I feel are set apart for a sacred purpose of quiet, inspiration, and revelation. It isn't an exhaustive list, but my hope is that seeing this list will remind you of your own or encourage you to create one.

- Home. Create a space in your home that is just for being still. A friend of mine uses her closet for this purpose. How many of us have prayed in our closets among our shoes and the colorful rainbow of our hanging clothes? I have a corner with a chair and a footstool. No music or outside noise is allowed in this area. I use it to read, write, pray, think, and study my scriptures.
- The temple. The celestial room is a common place for revelation and creating the negative space that makes room for heavenly communication. Lately, however, I've found the waiting area prior to performing initiatory work in the temple to be a beautiful place to reflect. Sometimes, if the temple is closed or if I just need centering, I find myself sitting in my parked car looking at the temple for the quiet I crave.
- Nature. Time spent in nature, near water and forest, is where I feel the most like myself with God.
- The bathtub. It seems funny to some, but for me, my bathtub is a sacred and holy place. I do a lot of praying and pleading alone at the end of the day in my tub. It is where I have solved many parenting dilemmas and have even had ideas for my writing.

Chapter Six
holy in our habits

"Heavenly Father has given each of us the capacity to become holy. . . . May our lives ever be a sacred offering, that we may stand before the Lord in the beauty of holiness."[51]

—Carol F. McConkie

Connie Bennion. You probably don't know her. I am so lucky that I do, but I am convinced that even though you don't know her, just reading her name will be a cool breath of peace to you because Connie Bennion is a holy woman. She is well educated secularly, theologically, and spiritually. She has lived a life of great devotion to everyone around her and especially to God. (Three days following my recent ward split, I stopped doing the dishes, sat down on my hardwood floor, and cried, wondering who would tell me who I am and how special I am to God if Connie wouldn't be around. She is that kind of wonderful.) And now, in the sunset of her life, Connie has become a caregiver to her husband. I love to watch as this small woman dotes on a tall man who, once distinct and

---

51 "The Beauty of Holiness," *Ensign*, May 2017.

> Holy women start their journeys to holiness by using their most precious commodity of time to become replete with Christlike attributes.

powerful in presence before his stroke, has become childlike in the best sense of the word, though sweet and still strong in his testimony. She takes his arm and calls him "my darling" with as much respect and dignity as she's ever offered him, even as he, in her words, "evaporates before her eyes." I've never seen anything so sacred—so set apart from the world. I want to be just like her. My life is full of holy women (and I believe my assertion that we are all holy.) Yet, some women stick out to me like the group of three aspen trees I saw on my hike last week whose trunks, topped with golden, fluttering leaves, dared to stand in stark contrast to the green spikes of thousands of pine trees. Three golden pillars in a wave of green. "Aspen-like women" are the women I want to emulate—those who stand in boldness amid a wave of sameness. Holy women start their journeys to holiness by using their most precious commodity of time to become replete with Christlike attributes. These women develop their holy attributes through their practice and possession of holy habits.

An action ceases to be a practice and becomes habit when it accomplishes two things: First, it is involuntary. Have you ever driven to your office or your child's school and realized that you can't recall having driven the past three blocks of your route?

Your brain has made the drive nearly involuntarily. Second, the action has become habit when it requires great effort to give it up. If it's easy to quit, it isn't yet a habit. If you are trying to develop a habit of scripture reading, simply completing a "Read the Book of Mormon in 30 days" challenge won't make your goal a habit. "Thirty-day challenges" may be impactful, but they aren't habit-forming. Completing a challenge like that would accomplish a goal but would not develop a habit. A goal is something with an end date, a finish line. A habit is an automatically acting part of you. Until it would be really hard on you to miss a day of scriptures, until not reading the scriptures would feel disconcerting, as if something were missing or lost, you have not formed a habit.

We've all heard that if we do something for twenty-one days, we'll be changed. Old research built on shallow studies used to indicate that this twenty-one-day principle had merit. The self-help world loved it. Telling someone they could develop a habit in under a month and showing them the five, seven, or ten easy steps to do or become something sold a lot of books. The latest research isn't as easy to sell. Dr. Phillippa Lally, and her team at the Cancer Research UK Health Behaviour Research Centre published an in-depth study about habit formation that suggests a much more realistic picture of the effort required to change. [52]

This team of researchers suggested that there is not one set number of days it takes to form a habit. Their research said that their participants' practiced action became a habit at between

52 Dr. Phillippa Lally, Cornelia H. M. van Jaarsveld Henry W. W. Potts, Jane Wardle. *How are habits formed: Modelling habit formation in the real world*, European Journal of Social Psychology, Volume 40, Issue 6, October 2010, 998–1009.

eighteen and two hundred forty-five days, with an average habit acquisition among all participants of sixty-six days. Nearly nine months of consistent effort for some and under a month for others, with a variety of factors contributing to the length of time needed for the habit's development. Likewise, habits that no longer serve us (formerly called "bad" habits) most of the time took even longer to cease being present in our lives.

Dr. Lally's research doesn't have to be discouraging if we can mentally discard one specific, predetermined outcome as the only thing of value and, instead, choose to see the very process of becoming as holy in and of itself. What if the process was as fulfilling as the end result? In my favorite of his talks, Elder Dallin H.

> What is important
> in the end is what
> we have become
> by our labors.

Oaks says, "What is essential is that our labors in the workplace of the Lord have caused us to become something. For some of us, this requires a longer time than for others. What is important in the end is what we have become by our labors."[53] We aren't failing! We are becoming! We are working to implement new holy habits and working to let go of those that no longer serve us.

The most exciting finding in Dr. Lally's research indicated that missing a day here and there in trying to form a habit

---

53 Dallin H. Oaks. "The Challenge to Become," *Ensign,* November 2000.

didn't matter! The research suggested that periodic failure had no impact on the eventual formation of the habit. It even went on to assert that if we believe our occasional slipup in habit formation has ruined our progress, it will be the belief itself that will derail our efforts. Conversely, if we believe that missing a day in our habit formation is part of our becoming, the time needed to develop a holy habit will not be impacted! "We must not give up hope," President Oaks goes on to say. "We must not stop striving. We are children of God, and it is possible for us to become what our Heavenly Father would have us become."

Here are some helpful practices in creating habits:

- Simplify. If your goal were to increase temple attendance and your current temple attendance was at a few times a year, you would be more successful to first create a habit of monthly attendance instead of a more difficult goal of weekly attendance. Don't worry! You can always set a new goal once this one has truly become a habit. Line upon line, sister, precept upon precept.

- Consistent, imperfect effort. Practicing habits consistently is important, but giving ourselves permission to be human without stigma, judgment, or the false idea that we are starting at square one is even more important. Remember, the study taught that consistency is most impactful when beginning to develop a desired habit, but periodic inconsistency didn't impact the ability to change ultimately.

- Desire. If we are implementing a habit out of obligation, we aren't very likely to fight through adversity to develop it. Our Heavenly Parents won't force us into holy habits.

Do you believe you can change? Do you want to? Part of Alma 32:27 reads, "Exercise a particle of faith, yea, even if ye can no more than desire to believe, *let this desire work in you*, even until ye believe in a manner that ye can give place for a portion of my words." Let this desire work in you till your desire becomes action and your action becomes habit.

- Creating context clues. Study on the topic of habit indicates that context clues are critical in forming habits. Circumstances, locations, and times are all helpful context clues. Here are some examples:
    - o Repeating the desired behavior under similar circumstances each day is a great context clue. *I write in my journal every day right before bed.*
    - o A context clue could use a specific location, such as, *I always read my scriptures in my favorite comfy chair.*
    - o Using time is one of the most helpful context clues: *our family studies our* Come, Follow Me *resources each Sunday at 7:30.*
- Prayer. Prayer is a helpful resource in the development of habits. This is ironic, seeing as how habitual, meaningful prayer is one of the habits I am working to develop. Yet, I know prayer is one of the most helpful tools in the development of habits. Prayer connects us to heaven and links us to God. It is a symbolic offering of our agency to align our will with His, allowing Him to give us the help we need.
- A holy habits team. I work better when I have people on my side to whom I can be accountable. People who

know me, love me, and are willing to call me out when necessary. (Yes, it's often necessary.) Forming holy habits is easier when I know someone else knows what I'm working on. While we'll only ever be successful forming a habit when we are doing it for ourselves and God, it does help to have support. I'm not forming a habit to gain the approval of anyone on my team, but I'm thankful they know that I'm working on it and love me enough to hold me accountable.

Here are some helpful practices in breaking habits that no longer serve us:

- Have desire, get rid of ambivalence. Breaking habits is hard work. It's helpful to really want it and to not be ambivalent about it. Do you have a large caffeinated diet soda every day with two shots of syrup flavoring and added cream? Are you working to break that habit? (Yeah, me neither. I was asking for a friend.) Telling yourself how bad your soda is for you and how horrible you are because you drink it will never increase your desire to change or get rid of your ambivalence. In fact, your self-loathing may be the very thing you hide behind to keep you from doing the hard work of breaking the habit. Instead, use positive self-talk and compassion for where you have been, and be very clear about where you want to go. Look to the future. Write a page or create a vision board about who you will be without the habit. Replace the habit you are trying to break with a positive habit you are trying to cultivate. Maybe my friend with the soda habit (who, remember, is definitely not me) would like to focus on developing a habit of drinking more water. What a great thing to focus on when the soda habit becomes difficult to break.

- Remove context clues. Getting rid of the context clues we talked about earlier can be helpful in eradicating habits. I used to have an app on my phone that became a sucker of time for me. (Have you ever experienced that mystical time vacuum? You open the phone, and when you're done, an hour of your life is gone? It's like a black-and-white sci-fi show from the 1960s.) When I wanted to break the habit of looking at the app, I deleted it and replaced its location on my shortcut screen with the icon to launch my Gospel Library app.

- Call on the Atonement. The Savior has promised that He will give rest to our burdened souls when we yoke ourselves to Him. It is so much easier to break a habit when I know I'm not alone and that my willpower has the power of heaven behind it. "Take my yoke upon you, and learn of me," Jesus says, "for I am meek and lowly in heart: and ye shall find rest unto your souls. For my yoke is easy, and my burden is light."[54]

- Seek professional help when needed. Some things are more than habits that no longer serve us. Some habits might have become addictions. If this is the case for you, don't be afraid. You aren't alone. The Savior knows you, loves you, and believes so much in your ability to change that He died for you. There is help, and you need to find it now. Your ecclesiastical leaders

---

54 Matthew 11:29–30.

can be a wonderful supporting role to professional counseling and/or medical support services. Your bishop might even be your first stop as you look into where to go for help. However, unless your bishop or stake president is a degree-holding therapist, social worker, or medical doctor, he is not qualified to help you. He can love you. He can support you. He can pray for you. He can help you manage your spiritual welfare. But he is not qualified to dispense medical or psychological advice that should be given by someone licensed in that field. The Church has a resource to use as a tool in addiction recovery and might be a good first place to go for support. You can find information at addictionrecovery.lds.org.

* * *

The research on habit formation takes the focus off the results and allows us to let go of the unrealistic "5 easy steps" or "21 easy days" to holiness, focusing instead on daily, individual efforts to become holier people. These daily efforts are the stuff of a holy life. Each day can be a little more set apart from the world, a little closer to God. Even if the practices we long to implement haven't become habit yet, each day of effort can be holy. Ultimately, there are but two things that, when woven together, have the ability to change us: first is our own will, and second is Christ's

> Each day can be a little more set apart from the world, a little closer to God.

Atonement. When we place our will at the feet of Christ and show Him through daily, imperfect action that we are striving to become holy, He will change our hearts! This is His Atonement at work on our behalf. He says, "A new heart also will I give you, and a new spirit will I put within you: and I will take away the stony heart out of your flesh, and I will give you an heart of flesh."[55]

There is a numberless list of holy habits each of us is working to attain. If you want to know where to start, be still. Offer a prayer. Listen. You'll know. These are some holy habits I've been working on and some of the reasons why. Our desired habits might cross paths, and they might not. You might find these to be the Sunday School answers, and there would certainly be an argument for that, but the truth is that I can't work on loftier habits till I've mastered these. They're the habits that most set my life aside for a sacred purpose.

Scripture study. I have read the scriptures each day since I was eighteen years old. The boy I was dating when I first started was called on a mission and asked me if, while he was gone, I would commit to reading the scriptures daily. (I know. You want to throw up a little. The scene is starting to sound very *Saturday's Warrior*-esque. As will a later scene in which I marry this missionary's best friend. Will it help to say he was "just a friend like those I count in dozens?" You can't blame me; I was a child of the '80s.) I agreed to his request and have maintained a daily scripture study for twenty years. A verse. Yes, many days, I read only one verse. It started as serious scripture study and unraveled from there. I'd like to develop a habit of daily scripture *study*, as in, more than a verse. However, I don't wish to diminish the power of that one verse.

---

55 Ezekiel 36:26.

If we want to develop a habit of scripture study, where would we start? In 2 Nephi 4:15, Nephi tells us that his soul "delighteth in the scriptures." So we would need to start where the scriptures can be a delight to our soul. Reading can't be a chore; it has to be engaging.

The great thing is the days are gone when scripture study meant only one thing. It used to be you, your scriptures, and a red pencil. Scripture study today can happen in so many ways. We can listen to audio versions on the way to work, buy beautifully designed study guides, join small study groups, take continuing education courses online or in person, buy an inexpensive copy of the Book of Mormon and write all over it, use popular apps for study, listen to podcasts about the scriptures—and these are just a few ideas! When we get creative with the way we invite the scriptures into our lives, studying them becomes fun and insightful in different ways.

And yet, there is something about you, your scriptures, and a red pencil, isn't there? Even though I read my scriptures the majority of the time on my phone now, there is something familiar and comforting about the way the pages of my paper scriptures turn. I find the scripture I'm searching for by looking for familiar colors of markings. And in the back is a sticker of a little girl on a swing that I put there when I was twelve years old. Opening the maroon leather, seeing the worn-away golden edges of each page, and feeling the weight of them in my lap feels like coming home. Find a quiet spot tonight. Take out your paper scriptures—maybe even a red pencil—and come home.

Temple worship. When all around us seems chaotic, there is hope in the peace of the temple. The ordinances we receive in the temple and the covenants we make have, more than anything else, the potential to create holiness inside of us. I can't pretend to

> When I visit the temple, I feel bound to
> my husband, to our children, to God.

teach you the depth of why the temple is holy. For that, I would recommend reading Elder Boyd K. Packer's definitive work *The Holy Temple*. I have been attending the temple for nearly twenty years, and there is still much I don't understand. I do know, however, that when I go to the temple, even if it is to sit on the grounds, I feel different. My heart softens. My head clears. I feel peace. When I visit the temple, I feel bound to my husband, to our children, to God. Remembering this eternal bind helps sustain me in the uproar of my life. As we make visiting the temple a habit, we can expect an increased ease to come into our lives.[56] Elder Renlund promises us, "When we gather our family histories and go to the temple on behalf of our ancestors, God fulfills promised blessings simultaneously on both sides of the veil."[57] I need these promised blessings. My family members need them. Just as much as my ancestors need to be saved, I need to be saved.

Within a week, I visited all the Church history sites (with the exception of Harmony, Pennsylvania), starting at the birthplace of

---

56 Where are my footnote lovers? In his talk, "Family History and Temple Work: Sealing and Healing," Elder Renlund identifies eleven blessings promised through our temple attendance. In studying the footnote for these eleven promised blessings, you will see that he studied twenty-three talks to find those promises. If you find yourself desiring to understand the promised blessings of temple attendance, read the talks listed in footnote 6, located at https://www.lds.org/general-conference/2018/04/family-history-and-temple-work-sealing-and-healing?lang=eng; accessed October 21, 2018.

57 Dale G. Renlund. "Family History and Temple Work: Sealing and Healing," *Ensign*, May 2018.

Joseph Smith, and working my way to Nauvoo, Illinois. Joseph and his family never stayed in any one place for long in those early years, experiencing bigotry that caused their expulsion from every place in which they tried to build up Zion. Everywhere they went, even places in which they were located only briefly, they first set out plans to build a temple, and cornerstones and never-actualized temple plans dot the east and Midwest. I think of the Saints building the temple in Nauvoo at the same time they were constructing wagon wheels to go west and wonder how I can pass a temple every day as if it is commonplace. My normal, my refuge, my healing place are thanks in part to the early Saints' holy sacrifice. How can I not work to make my regular attendance a habit?

Increased temple attendance is an intentional practice. Treating time I set aside for the temple as non-negotiable has helped me be successful in actually getting there. But if you struggle to meet your goal, asking a friend to be a temple partner could be helpful. My friend Michelle and I attend the temple more consistently when we hold each other accountable.

Worship. The recent shift in our thinking takes worship out of our churches and temples primarily and makes worship less of what we *do* and more of who we *are*. Developing daily habits of worship in our own way helps us be different from the world around us and more able to be used in the service of others.

We can determine how our families worship. In our family, music is an integral part of our worship. Holiness is singing hymns by the fireplace on Sunday nights, with the glow of the fire and lamps as our only source of light. My oldest harmonizes, my youngest adds his own sweet voice. It isn't perfect, but it's perfect. You know what I mean. It's how we do worship; it's how we do holy. In this form of worship, we set ourselves apart and offer the week before us as an offering to heaven.

Taking the sacrament. The day I was baptized is forever etched in my memory. I can still clearly recall the feeling of coming out of the water and most especially the feeling when I was invited to receive the Holy Ghost into my life during my confirmation. In the tabernacle on Temple Square, I was baptized with both water and fire. And now, when I take the sacrament, I try to think about the power I felt that day. I try to internalize that partaking of the sacrament and taking Christ's name upon me are renewals of this strength. Simply taking the sacrament is easy; it's already habit. The habit I'm developing now is the ability to feel the power of my baptismal covenant and my confirmation just as intently as I did that day in 1988.

Making the sacrament a holy habit will be different for each of us as we strive to take that fifteen minutes of our week and set it so far apart that it sanctifies us for the week to come.

Prayer. What are holy prayers like? Honest prayers are holy prayers. Prayers that pray for things and people specifically and by name. Prayers that are full of gratitude. Prayers that ask where God wants us to go, then take action on the answer.

Reserving time each day for private, specific prayers is essential in making prayer habitual. Amulek gives us ideas of how to develop a holy habit of prayer in his soliloquy to the Zoramites, delivered on the hill of Antionum in Alma 34:

> Therefore may God grant unto you, my brethren, that ye may begin to exercise your faith unto repentance, that ye begin to call upon his holy name, that he would have mercy upon you; Yea, cry unto him for mercy; for he is mighty to save. Yea, humble yourselves, and continue in prayer unto him. Cry

unto him when ye are in your fields, yea, over all your flocks. Cry unto him in your houses, yea, over all your household, both morning, mid-day, and evening. Yea, cry unto him against the power of your enemies. Yea, cry unto him against the devil, who is an enemy to all righteousness. Cry unto him over the crops of your fields, that ye may prosper in them. Cry over the flocks of your fields, that they may increase. But this is not all; ye must pour out your souls in your closets, and your secret places, and in your wilderness. Yea, and when you do not cry unto the Lord, let your hearts be full, drawn out in prayer unto him continually for your welfare, and also for the welfare of those who are around you.[58]

Meditation. Meditation has a lot of definitions, but to me, its best definition is "sacred mental space I create to simply exist as a daughter of God." Meditation isn't *doing* anything; it is the intentional absence of doing. In yoga we call it "watching the watcher." Thoughts might come in. We don't judge them; we just watch them pass by. Time spent in this place leads to a deep, spiritual connection and understanding of my divine nature. A habit of meditation before and after prayer will add to the stillness that invites us to receive personal revelation.

Learning. "The glory of God is intelligence, or, in other words, light and truth."[59] Habitual learning, with the goal of setting our lives further apart from the world, doesn't have to

---

58 Alma 34:17–27.
59 Doctrine and Covenants 93:36.

happen solely in a classroom; it can happen anytime we open ourselves to receive new knowledge. Any place we learn, grow, and progress is a sacred space, and anytime is the right time.

Developing a habit of learning can be as simple as listening to audiobooks as you carpool, taking a continuing education class, studying resources on a specific topic, or reading out of the best books. It can also be as in-depth as earning collegiate-level degrees, learning a trade, or becoming a gospel scholar.

Our culture used to send the message to us women that our learning was a backup plan—something we would need just in case. Our habits of learning, whether through formal education or not, shouldn't be our plan B; they should be plan A. Learning is part of our divine nature as daughters of a Heavenly Mother. Dr. Eva Witesman's June 27, 2017, BYU devotional address entitled "Women and Education: A Future Only God Could See for You" was groundbreaking as she spoke about education for women as worthy simply for the sake of learning, not as a backup plan. She said, "Our learning is of value not only if we become mothers or workers, church leaders or community activists. We are of value because of our divine heritage and because of what will one day be our divine inheritance. Our value is not merely instrumental. It is intrinsic. And our learning is not merely instrumental. It is essential."

> Any place we learn, grow, and progress is a sacred space, and anytime is the right time.

Inspired by Dr. Witesman's address, I saved my

pennies and purchased a piece of her artwork entitled "Totality." It is a mixed-media art piece. She used acrylic paint, plaster, and enamel to create a 3-D set of angel wings mounted on a painted black canvas, with a copper ring encircling the wings. I love it. Each time I look at it in my office, I am reminded of my sacred and godlike ability to enrich myself with continual learning.

We know that when we leave this life, we take little with us. One of our precious eternal possessions is our knowledge. In developing habits of learning, we step just a little bit closer to the holiness we seek.

* * *

Attempts to create or abandon habits will come over time, and often, we don't see ourselves maturing in our habits. It is easy to see where we lack but harder to acknowledge the ways in which we've grown. When I am a few decades older, I hope another woman will have noticed Christ in me just as I noticed it in my friend and gospel sister Connie. I hope this holiness of character will have been formed from my hard-earned holy habits. I hope the woman I am will have been impactful enough in bringing people to Christ that this other sister will have cause to sit upon her kitchen floor and weep over the loss of my constant influence. It's a worthy goal to strive for. God bless you and me as we work for eighteen days, two hundred forty-five days, or an entire lifetime to cultivate the habits that will become attributes that will set our lives apart as sacred, as holy.

Chapter Seven
to be like thee: nurturing holy attributes

"As we strive to acquire His divine attributes in our lives, we become different than we were, through the Atonement of Christ the Lord, and our love for all people increases naturally."[60]

—Ulisses Soares

While in high school, I had a dream that I went to a party with a friend. Music played, and groups of people we knew were chatting and laughing together. Someone came in the door, and my friend and I both turned to look. Not recognizing the man, I turned my attention back to the party and noticed that my friend was no longer by my side. Looking back to see where she had gone, I found her kneeling at the feet of the stranger who had come through the door. She was crying with joy, "Master, Master, Master." In my dream, a realization came over me. This man was the Savior, and I hadn't recognized Him. I stepped back into the crowd, full of remorse that Christ had come and no one, including me,

---

60 "One in Christ," *Ensign*, November 2018.

was even paying attention. I wanted to run to Him, but I was afraid, so instead, I hid where He wouldn't see me watching Him. That is where the dream ended.

I woke up sad and worried. My teenage self was confused at the dream. Why hadn't I been one to fall at Christ's feet? Why hadn't I recognized Him, and why, when I did realize who it was, did I not follow my desire to run to Him? The saddest part of the dream to me both then and now is that, though there was no consequential reason for why I should have removed myself from His presence, because I was worthy in every way. Yet, when the choice came to step forward or backward, I stepped back. Perhaps I thought I wasn't good enough, but even if that had been true, it should not have disqualified me from running to my Savior. Do we know we are enough to step toward Christ? We are enough, not because of anything we have or haven't done to prove ourselves but because we are His.

The lesson of this decades-old dream is one I think of all the time: how can I live my life in such a way that I will recognize the Savior when He comes again. How will I know Him, and how will He know me? How can I believe that in spite of my humanity, I am worthy of His love?

Instead of stepping back into the crowd and watching Christ from afar, I have to develop the courage to step, in all of my imperfection, toward Him, believing that God's grace is sufficient for me.[61] I have to set my life apart. I have to make it holy by developing attributes that make me more Christlike.

As women seeking a holier life, we want to be like Him. The more we, as women with a desire to be like Christ, develop

---

61 See Moroni 10:32.

these holy habits and attributes, the more His image becomes imprinted upon our countenance.[62]

How are you feeling about this? Talking about attributes of a holy life makes me a little nervous. Sometimes at church, when all of the beautiful and "right" things are being said, my perfectionism kicks in, and I shut down. I get that yucky idea that wrongly tells me that if I do everything just right, I am worthy to be loved and that if I don't, I'm not. I look at words like *forgiving, loving,* and *obedient,* and I start to panic and shut down in the false notion that because I can never be perfectly loving, perfectly forgiving, or perfectly obedient, I'm not ever going to be worthy of His love. I take metaphorical steps back into the crowd so that He won't see me and find me lacking, even though the thing I want to do most is run to Him. In this place, my mind tells me that reading and writing about these things must be for the perfect people, not for me. I'm the one who swore at her dog yesterday and who really wants to ignore that text asking me to substitute teach in Primary. I'm tempted to think that I'm not holy and never will be.

It takes a lot of practice to be able to shut down my untrue thoughts when I get in this type of downward spiral. Here's the thing: we are about to talk about holy attributes. I don't want you to be miserable, and I don't want you to skip the chapter, be frustrated, or feel anxious because you aren't perfectly any of these things. Sister, I know you aren't! And guess who else knows you aren't? Christ. He knows! And so does Heavenly Father, Heavenly Mother, your ancestors, and the angels by your side. We all know, and none of us cares that you aren't

---

62 See Alma 5:14.

perfect. In fact, we see all of your imperfect efforts to try to live a holier life, and we think they are awesome!

Letting go of perfectionism doesn't mean that we stop trying to be better people. We still try! But we do it with our hearts in the right place, knowing the Atonement is there for us when we fall and that because of Christ, we are able to be holier every day. I know it takes vulnerability, but I challenge you to read about each of these attributes, and instead of obsessing over all the aspects of the attribute that *you are not*, lean into the nuances that you already *are*.

Validating what you are already doing to make yourself holy will inspire belief that you can do a little more. If you read this chapter with a focus on making yourself a list of all the things you should be but are not in order to be holy, you won't do anything to attain any of them. Shame is not from God. It is not a motivational tool and will never change your heart. You can succeed, on the other hand, at separating yourself from the world as you begin to appreciate the holy attributes you already have and take time to feel about yourself the way Christ feels about you. Doing so will bring you assurance that you are of infinite worth to your Savior, which will give you hope that as you strive to develop holy attributes, you are taking sacred, vulnerable steps toward Christ.

If feelings of inadequacy, shame, perfectionism, fear, or any other triggering feeling comes in, don't panic; just observe the feeling. Maybe say aloud, "Lord, I feel_____ about_____." Observe and write down the thoughts, feelings, and questions that come up. Your eternal life is in process. You will always be growing toward a holier you.

The following are but a few of the many Christlike attributes we can nurture. I hope that illustrating these few attributes as holy will help you see attributes you want to nurture within yourself and attributes you already possess, and that in so doing, you will see yourself clearly as set apart from the world for sacredness just as you are in this very moment.

Holy Attribute: Obedient. My bishop recently said that any blessing in your life can be directly related to an aspect of the gospel in which you were obedient. As he said those words, I thought about what I consider my greatest blessings and readily agreed with him. Each of my blessings has come from obedience to a commandment. In Alma 57:21, Helaman tells us about the stripling warriors and points out that as they obeyed with exactness

> The Lord Himself said that He is "bound when ye do what I say."

and that through their faith, they were given desired blessings. Helaman says, "Yea, and they did obey and observe to perform every word of command with exactness; yea, and even according to their faith it was done unto them."

As we strive to be holier and attain blessings in our mortal lives, we would be wise to be obedient. The Lord Himself said that He is "bound when ye do what I say," yet He goes on to add that "when ye do not what I say, ye have no promise."[63] When we do what we are asked, we can expect that the Lord will fulfill His end of the bargain. Exact obedience is not blind

---

63 Doctrine and Covenants 82:10.

obedience or submission. Obedience is not a virtue when not coming from agency and an open heart. Dr. Jennifer Finlayson-Fife says, "When submission is a virtue, it's an active choice to yield to something because you think it will create the greater good. It's not driven by fear; it's driven by moral courage."[64] It's a different way than many of us have thought about obedience, but it is vitally important that we treasure our agency and submit our own will. This is a higher form of obedience than what we learned in the world or even in our culture. It's a way of viewing this holy attribute that we perhaps don't consider enough. We set ourselves apart as we, of our own will, obey the commandments with an open and honest heart, believing that doing so will bring light to our lives and take us closer to Christ.

Holy Attribute: Willing to Stand Alone. Living a holy life will always require you to, at various times throughout your life, stand alone in your convictions. When we are who we say we are and do what we say we will do, we are living in our integrity. The classic Personal Progress book for the young women provides them with this definition: "Integrity: I will have the moral courage to make my actions consistent with my knowledge of right and wrong." The holy life can be lonely. This loneliness can feel unsettling and can make us look for a group of people to calm our feelings. It is tempting to give in to what sociologists call "groupthink," a dangerous practice in which people's desire for harmony and the ability fit in among a group leads them to be silent as to their honest feelings—leading to irrational group decision making. When in groupthink mode, we often say and do what we wouldn't normally. We espouse ideals that aren't ours in the name of fitting in. However, it is

64 Jennifer Finlayson-Fife on podcast "The Christian Doormat," moderated by Sharrae Phelps.

those with the courage to stand for what they believe, even if it means standing alone, who change the world.

In one of my favorite books, *Standing for Something* by President Gordon B. Hinckley, he notes that "what we desperately need today on all fronts—in our homes and communities, in schoolrooms and boardrooms, and certainly throughout society at large—are leaders, men and women who are willing to stand for something. We need people who are honest; who are willing to stand up for decency, truth, integrity, morality and law and order; who respond to their consciences even when it is unpopular to do so—perhaps especially when it is unpopular to do so."[65] His advice is solid and even more applicable today than when he first gave it.

We must be prepared to stand up in the world among strangers. We must, at times, stand alone in our community, Church congregation, family, and amongst our closest friends. Learning to stand for what we believe in a non-polarizing way that offers love and compassion to others, especially those closest to us, is a skill we have to acquire over time and practice. I've failed. Many times. But I keep trying, and you can keep trying too. As you find the courage to stand alone, you might find that you won't be alone for long. Inspired by your fortitude, others will be inspired to join you.

The world is getting louder. Everywhere we go, we are told to choose a side. And once we do, we are told what people on that side are expected to think. When we can stand for our own personal beliefs, we might feel alone, but we will actually belong. To ourselves and, ultimately, to God. Dr. Brené Brown's research says, "True belonging is the spiritual practice of believing in and

65 Gordon B. Hinckley. *Standing for Something: 10 Neglected Virtues That Will Heal Our Hearts and Homes* [Random House, 2000], 167.

belonging to yourself so deeply that you can share your most authentic self with the world and find sacredness in both being a part of something and standing alone in the wilderness. True belonging doesn't require you to change who you are; it requires you to be who

> When we turn toward our Father, we turn away from the things that hold us back.

you are."[66] We are daughters of Heavenly Parents. Even when we stand alone, we never stand alone.

Holy Attribute: Repentant. Do you know what repentance is . . . what it *really* is? It isn't a punishment. It's a course correction. When we sin, we are taking ourselves away from God. Repentance is recognizing that we are off course, renouncing whatever it is that has kept us off course, and doing what we need to do to get back on course, pointed again toward God. Elder Dale G. Renlund points out that repentance "in Swedish . . . is *omvänd*, which simply means 'to turn around.'"[67] If we are turning toward something, we are turning away from something else. When we turn toward our Father, we turn away from the things that hold us back. In order to repent, we leave behind anything coming between us and our path to God. The Atonement is the force that turns us. It seems so simple, so astoundingly simple! Yet, it

---

66   Brené Brown. *Braving the Wilderness: The Quest for True Belonging and the Courage to Stand Alone.,* Audiobook chapter two, 16 minutes, 47 seconds—17 minutes, 10 seconds.

67   Dale G. Renlund. "Repentance: A Joyful Choice," *Ensign,* November 2016.

isn't always without hurt. The godly sorrow that accompanies repentance is painful. But it's a holy pain. It's the kind of pain that frees us from the sinful leashes that tether us and keep us stuck. It hurts to be seen for what we have been, and it hurts to know the pain we caused the Savior, who ultimately takes it all upon Himself, but it's beautiful too. Isn't it? To be seen and still loved? I imagine the Savior standing in between my sin and me, loosing the tethers, then placing His hands on my shoulders and physically turning me back toward our Father and Mother. The process feels hard, long, and then sudden. This "turning of the heart and will to God"[68] is an act of holiness.

When we repent, He "remembers [our sin] no more."[69] Do we let our sin make that sacred transition from mistake to life lesson? We diminish the holiness of repentance when we don't believe we have been forgiven and continue to berate ourselves for the people we once were. Once you're free, be free. Christ says, "Behold, I am the law, and the light. Look unto me, and endure to the end, and ye shall live; for unto him that endureth to the end will I give eternal life."[70] Look to me, He says. Look to me—repent—and live.

Holy Attribute: Forgiving. One of my traits I appreciate is that I am willing to see when I am wrong and strive to repent. I'm good at laying my sin, my missteps, my needed improvements, at our Savior's feet, yet, forgiveness is hard for me. It isn't that I don't believe people can change. I do. It's that I'm afraid of what will happen if I lay down the burden of another's wrong against me.

Even when we are willing to lay down our own sins at Christ's feet, are we willing to lay the weight of others' sins in

68 Bible Dictionary, "Repentance."
69 Doctrine and Covenants 58:42.
70 3 Nephi 15:9.

front of Him as well? Sometimes the hurt others bring to us with the use of their agency is so heavy that we carry it because we are afraid. We think if we put it down, no one will hurt for our experiences—our offenders certainly aren't hurting. So if we're not suffering for the wrongs against us, who will be a witness to our pain? And if we give our pain to the Savior, we don't get to be wounded anymore. If I'm not wounded, am I somehow condoning another's wrongs against me?

While on the path of forgiveness in a particularly difficult situation, I took great comfort in the words of Desmond TuTu, a South African Anglican cleric and human rights activist: "Forgiveness does not relieve someone of responsibility for what they have done. Forgiveness does not erase accountability. It is not about turning a blind eye or even turning the other cheek. It is not about letting someone off the hook or saying it is okay to do something monstrous. Forgiveness is simply about understanding that every one of us is both inherently good and inherently flawed. Within every hopeless situation and every seemingly hopeless person lies the possibility of transformation."[71] Our offenders will be held accountable by a perfect judge. That has to be enough for us because forgiving was never about them. It was always about us and our freedom. Let the Savior worry about our offenders. We forgive for our own peace.

It's time to move on and be free. We say we want to be healed. But do we? Forgiving means we become accountable for our own lives. No more excuses. No more blame. For those of us used to carrying the burden of another's sin, sometimes for many years, putting the burden down can be a terrifying prospect! But I have a secret. You can do it. I know that forgiving

71 *The Book of Forgiving: The Fourfold Path for Healing Ourselves and Our World* [Harper One, 2013].

can be the hardest work you will ever do. And the path might be long. But when you find yourself free, it will be worth the rockiest of paths.

Forgiveness is not just a phrase you say and then it is done. "I forgive you" isn't all that's required. Freedom in the form of forgiveness is first found in honoring your story. This will require a partnership with the Savior and might even necessitate help from others: therapists, ecclesiastical leaders, confidantes, maybe even law enforcement and the judicial system.

Freedom through forgiveness is uneasy at first. It feels like learning to walk. And just like learning to walk, you're going to fall a lot, maybe your whole life, and still get back up again. Stop telling yourself that forgiveness is a one-and-done event. It, like repentance, is a constant turning back. Forgiveness may have to happen more than once. More than twice. More than hundreds of times. Sometimes, even many times for the same offense.

In a Sunday Relief Society meeting about forgiveness, I was fidgety. I hated lessons about forgiveness. In spite of my best efforts, I found myself unable to forgive a specific offense. Year after year, I would think I had forgiven only to have the situation arise again. I'd read the inspirational books about people suffering horrific things and frankly forgiving those who'd hurt them. I thought I must be a bad forgiver. I had tried to frankly forgive . . . probably hundreds of times. Each time, I'd inevitably find myself circling back to my wounds and feeling like I was missing it all somehow. It was in this place that I found myself during this personally significant Relief Society lesson. Sad and ready for the meeting to be over, I saw my friend Anne raise her hand. "What if," she said, "when Jesus is saying that we have to forgive seventy times seven times, He isn't talking about different events? What if He is talking about forgiving seventy times seven times for the same thing?" My mind was blown. Could it be possible that Christ knew we would have to revisit forgiveness for a single offense? Was it possible that forgiveness was more of a practice than a one-time event? This experience changed my entire perspective. I began to be at peace when I felt the need to forgive again. *Just part of my seventy times seven*, I'd think. When my perspective shifted and my self-judgment left, I was able to honor my experiences from a place of love and compassion.

Now, I occasionally find myself living a perfectly normal day when something happens that will remind me of the pain I once carried. I notice myself walking back to the feet of the Savior and trying to pick my load of pain back up—my heavy load made of another's wrongs. I have to remind myself that I've already put that down. It never belonged to me in the first place. So I take my hands off of it again. And when I do, Christ is always there—happy to take it from me and remind me of who I am. I've stopped calling myself a bad forgiver, and I've embraced the need to honor my story and forgive again as a beautiful sign of my devotion. I was willing to forgive again. That is no small thing. It's a holy thing.

"How great, how glorious, how complete Redemption's grand design, where justice, love, and mercy meet in harmony divine!"[72]

Holy Attribute: Grateful. If I were asked to write a dictionary, which I would never be asked to do, as my verbosity tends to get the best of me, here is how I would define *gratitude*:

---

72 "How Great the Wisdom and the Love," *Hymns*, no. 195.

gratitude is the act of stepping outside our circumstances, good or bad, with deep appreciation for the privilege it is to exist. Gratitude is the fastest road to holiness. In any circumstance, there is always something to be grateful for. We live in an era of entitlement, when gratitude is saying "thanks" when we get what we want. Gratitude is so much more than that. True gratitude encompasses not only all that you have but also all that you are, all that you have been, and all that you will be. Elder Uchtdorf says, "It is difficult to develop a spirit of gratitude if our thankfulness is only proportional to the number of blessings we can count."[73]

True gratitude is available to us even through trials. To illustrate this, I look to the woman I was fifteen years ago. I love her and have great compassion for her (she definitely had fewer wrinkles), but I have become such a different person—more like the woman I hope to someday be. As I look to the past, much of my growth has come from my difficulties. How then can I be grateful for who I have become without being grateful for the trials? I couldn't. I have to be grateful for the challenges too. Gratitude has the power to forge a resilience inside us that nothing can take away.

Recently, I woke up with anxiety at around four in the morning. The familiar speeding of my heart and feeling a loss of breath caused me to be instantly and totally awake. At first, I was frustrated. I'd gotten little sleep the night before, and anxiety meant that this night, I would get even less. In spite of my incredible disappointment, I tried in the moment to take my mind to things for which I am grateful: *My husband's sleeping sighs. Sheets that I love. A warm house.* There was so much to be grateful

---

73 Dieter F. Uchtdorf. "Grateful in Any Circumstances," *Ensign*, May 2014.

for. Did it work? Yes. But, maybe not in a storybook type of way. It depends on how you describe success. Did my anxiety disappear? No. Did I go back to sleep? No. But it did bring me a sense of peace and a sliver of hope within the

> If we are looking for gratitude to exist only in the absence of emotional discomfort, we will miss out on much of life's capacity for holiness.

anxious moments, allowing me to experience a challenging circumstance in a holy and almost noble way. I got out of bed exhausted the next morning but with gratitude in my heart. If we are looking for gratitude to exist only in the absence of emotional discomfort, we will miss out on much of life's capacity for holiness.

"What is the one thing that people who can fully lean into joy have in common?" researcher and author Brené Brown asks. "Gratitude. They practice gratitude. It's not an attitude of gratitude, it's an actual practice."[74]

Begin today to practice gratitude. President James E. Faust called gratitude a "saving principle"[75] for its ability to open our eyes to the mercy and wonder of God's love all around us. It's there for the taking if we will but see it.

74 *Dare to Lead: Brave Work. Tough Conversations. Whole Hearts* (October 2018), Audiobook, chapter 25, 3 minutes 35 seconds.
75 James E. Faust. "Gratitude as a Saving Principle," *Ensign,* May 1990.

Holy Attribute: Loving. Luke 10:27: "Thou shalt love the Lord thy God with all thy heart, and with all thy soul, and with all thy strength, and with all thy mind; and thy neighbor as thyself." There is one aspect of love in which the world is collectively tanking. We aren't seeking to be one. We are divided, and we believe that if we show love or compassion to someone else, we are being disloyal to our ideals. Loving people who are different from us is fundamental to what it means to be a disciple of Christ and to espouse the attribute of love as one that we possess. Love is a commandment: "A new commandment I give unto you, That ye love one another; as I have loved you, that ye also love one another. By this shall all men know that ye are my disciples, if ye have love one to another."[76]

Go with me to 1838. It was a year of trial and devastation for the Latter-day Saints. Their prophet was newly imprisoned in Liberty Jail, and Governor Lilburn Boggs had issued an extermination order authorizing the use of deadly force against any Mormon. "The Mormons must be treated as enemies," the order said, "and must be exterminated or driven from the state if necessary."[77] Some had even suffered a massacre at Hawn's Mill in which fifteen men and two boys were murdered, thirteen people were injured, and many women suffered sexual assault but are not historically noted as victims due to the silence of the time in which they lived. It was this group of battered and broken Saints who fled across the great Mississippi River to the small town of Quincy, Illinois. Approximately five thousand Latter-day Saint refugees washed

76 John 13:34–35.
77 *Church History in the Fulness of Times Student Manual*, 2nd ed. (Church Educational System manual, 2003), 199–201.

up, literally, on the banks of the town of only fifteen hundred people. Having heard the rumors of these people and being without resources, it would have been easy for the good people of Quincy to turn their backs and close the doors on these strangers. That isn't what happened though. Instead, a poor and already-spread-thin people took these five thousand Saints, Emma Smith being one of them, into their homes in the middle of winter. It is said that the good people of Quincy "donated liberally, the merchants vying with each other as to which could be the most liberal."[78] When the Saints were recovered as physically and as emotionally as could be expected, they said goodbye to Quincy and made their way to Nauvoo, where they built a glorious city of industry and beauty. They never forgot the goodness of the people there, but soon the lives of the Saints would again turn to tragedy, and they'd be forced to cross the Mississippi, this time toward the west, leaving in the dust of the plains the story of their time in Quincy.

I myself hadn't heard the story of the people of Quincy, Illinois, until the summer of 2018 while visiting Nauvoo. My family and I listened to the story told from the mouth of an Idaho farmer turned Nauvoo missionary. He recounted the tale as we took a wagon ride on dirt roads of the old Saints' farms. The horses' hooves smacked dust into the air, and my tears from the emotion of the missionary's stories made mud from the dust on my face.

Prior to Nauvoo, we visited Hawn's Mill, where, in the beauty of a pristine and silent field, I could almost hear juxtaposed ghostly cries of those early Saints left to mourn the dead. They were the long-gone cries of women who had buried their husbands and

---

78 Newsroom, "Quincy" July 5, 2002.

sons by dumping the bodies into an empty well before fleeing. These people had been and were, no doubt, expecting to be met by any number of bigoted and hateful acts. Yet, they were met in Quincy with love.

What then? Are we not called to do the same? If God worked through the people of Quincy in behalf of the Saints, can He not work through the Saints on behalf of all people in our time? Does He not expect us to love our brothers and sisters as we were once loved?

> For I was an hungred, and ye gave me meat: I was thirsty, and ye gave me drink: I was a stranger, and ye took me in: Naked, and ye clothed me: I was sick, and ye visited me: I was in prison, and ye came unto me. Then shall the righteous answer him, saying, Lord, when saw we thee an hungred, and fed thee? or thirsty, and gave thee drink? When saw we thee a stranger, and took thee in? or naked, and clothed thee? Or when saw we thee sick, or in prison, and came unto thee? And the King shall answer and say unto them, Verily I say unto you, Inasmuch as ye have done it unto one of the least of these my brethren, ye have done it unto me.[79]

Part of loving others is refraining from judgment. I used to think I was very good at this. I have a passionate "to each their own" philosophy of living my life. I'm not a judgmental person. Or so I thought. In the past few years, I have become painfully

---

79 Matthew 25:35–40.

aware that I am just as judgmental as anyone, if not worse. I judge the judgers! If you are like me and listen to someone make a comment in a Church meeting, then say in your mind, "Oh my, that person is so judgmental. I'm grateful to be enlightened and free of judgment," then you actually aren't free of judgment. President Thomas S. Monson offered me a loving reproach when I read his words from an October 2010 conference talk. He said, "Do [our] differences tempt us to judge one another? Mother Teresa, a Catholic nun who worked among the poor in India most of her life, spoke this profound truth: 'If you judge people, you have no time to love them.' . . . I ask: can we love one another, as the Savior has commanded, if we judge each other? And I answer—with Mother Teresa: no, we cannot."[80]

Let me tell you a story of two judgmental people. And yes, I type with a sigh and a blushing face—one of them is me.

I have an especially sacred place in my heart for our gay sisters and brothers. I have learned from those I love that being gay, especially within the membership of the Church, isn't easy. When I think of those who are gay and faithfully trying to live by the gospel standards, I am awed and humbled. Do we realize what they are being asked to do? Come to church every Sunday, where they will hear about families. Keep covenants that will keep them celibate in this life. Grow old without a companion or choose to enter into the challenging world of mixed-orientation marriage. Yet, trying their best to hold their testimony and their identities as gay people, they come to church week after week. This devotion should be met with awe in addition to absolute, complete, and total respect.[81] Instead, this devotion is

80   Thomas S. Monson. "Charity Never Faileth," *Ensign*, November 2010.
81   May I suggest this amazing book: *That We May Be One: A Gay Mormon's Perspective on Faith and Family* by Tom Christofferson.

often met with condemnation, misunderstanding, and isolation. Straight members of the Church have to do better with our gay sisters and brothers. Elder M. Russell Ballard tells us, "We need to listen to and understand what our LGBT brothers and sisters are feeling and experiencing. Certainly, we must do better than we have done in the past so that all members feel they have a spiritual home where their brothers and sisters love them and where they have a place to worship and serve the Lord."[82]

A few years ago, a brother stood at the pulpit in our congregation during a fast and testimony meeting and condemned our gay brothers and sisters with homophobic slurs, misused scriptures, and hateful rhetoric.

I was full of what I thought to be righteous indignation. Looking around me, I saw members of my congregation whose sons, sisters, and friends were gay. All of them looked shaken. I was enraged. I waited for someone to do something. No one did. Finally, I stood and audibly said, "I don't have to listen to this." From the middle of the row in the middle of the congregation, I pushed past each person in my row and stormed out the door to brood by the bishop's office. As our bishop wasn't present that day, I waited for one of his counselors and continued to fume. When the meeting ended, I asked to speak to one of the counselors in the clerk's office, and I let that poor counselor have it. This sweet man, this volunteer who has done so much for my family was the recipient of my wrath. I unleashed fury, the likes of which are rarely seen in a clerk's office.

Immediately, I felt bad. The Spirit was nowhere to be found, but I felt justified. It wasn't until years later that I saw how my behavior that day had not "knit [anyone's] hearts together in

82 "Questions and Answers." Brigham Young University Devotional, November 14, 2017, speeches.byu.ed.

love."[83] My behavior had also been hateful and divisive. It hadn't helped my gay brothers and sisters. No one felt closer to the Savior because of my public stand. My behavior had just made it clear that there were two sides: the aggressive testimony bearer's and mine. Ironic, isn't it, considering the only real opinion that matters is the Savior's?

Thankfully, years of growth taught me how Christ and God want their people to obey the second great commandment to love one another. Jesus says, "They all may be one; as thou, Father, art in me, and I in thee, that they also may be one in us."[84] They want us to be one, united in common goals. "And the Lord called his people Zion, because they were of one heart and one mind, and dwelt in righteousness; and there was no poor among them."[85] Are we not all seeking Zion? Don't we long for our communities, churches, and homes to be Zion-like? To be of one heart and one mind, we must dig beneath our differences and find that which ties us together in Christ. We must love people wherever they are in their progression. We must suspend judgment. We must embrace grace. This does not mean that we must espouse each other's ideals, take the same stance on every issue, or excuse someone's behavior. We will never agree with everyone all the time. And we were never meant to. Following the commandments means we are required to look beneath the surface and find the things that make us the same. I am not saying I should have

> Are we not all seeking Zion?

---

83 Colossians 2:2.
84 John 17:21.
85 Moses 7:18.

stayed silent that day. I do not excuse the testimony bearer's hateful behavior. Nor do I excuse mine. Both were full of judgment. Both were wrong. What I should have done that day is try better to understand my brother and stand for my beliefs in a more appropriate and loving manner. I determined that next time, if there is a next time, I would be a disciple of Jesus Christ, one who unites rather than divides.

Three years later, fast and testimony meeting came again. This brother again stood. Just as before, he began a tirade against gay people. And just as before, fury and judgment arose within my soul. But this time something happened. I was able to see that I was judging a judger. This time, I felt no righteous indignation. Throughout his long testimony, I prayed, my heart breaking with each of the testimony's harsh declarations. Not able to listen anymore, remembering how I did not want to act but not knowing how a disciple of Christ *should* act, I began to read the scriptures. I opened and read "And [Christ] will take upon him their infirmities, that his bowels may be filled with mercy, according to the flesh, that he may know according to the flesh how to succor his people according to their infirmities."[86] I was comforted with the immediate thought that Christ knows how to succor my sisters and brothers who are gay. Yet, just as quickly, an unexpected conversation with the Spirit unfolded:

"Why are you angry with this brother?" the Spirit impressed upon my mind.

To which, I replied, "I am angry because he is having such a hard time loving people who are different than he is."

The thought then came, "Are *you* not having a hard time loving someone who thinks differently than you?" I was humbled

86 Alma 7:12.

and silent as this next thought came: "Christ will succor His gay children, but He also knows how to succor this brother too."

A rush of love for this brother came over me, and a list of possibilities that gave me compassion ran through my mind. They included thoughts like, "What if he's never known someone who is gay? What if he himself is gay? What if he was taught this behavior? What if it is possible for my love to help teach him a better way?" The possibility that any of these "what if" questions could be true filled me with compassion and, dare I say, love.

He ended his testimony, and I, with scriptures in hand, stood to bear mine. In full disclosure, my husband was terrified and looked at me with eyes that said, "Please, do not do whatever it is you are about to do." (Poor man. Eternity's a long time.) I think many in the ward might have had the same worry as they saw me stand. They didn't need to worry though. This time, I bore my testimony of the Atonement. I read Alma 7:12 and testified of a loving Christ who knows how to succor His people. I bore testimony of the hope I have in Christ, that through Him, we can learn to love people who are different than we are and think differently than we do. I witnessed that we are not separate; we are one.

I sat down in complete shock at what had just taken place—I had been softened. This brother and I had become one. Who would have thought it could be? And to this day, when I see this brother in the community, I make it a point to smile and chat. I feel love for him.

On September 18, 2018, Carolina Núñez gave an address at Brigham Young University's weekly devotional.[87] In the

---

87 Carolina Núñez. "Loving Our Neighbors" [Brigham Young University devotional, Sept. 18, 2018], speeches.byu.ed.

speech, Dean Núñez described a visit to Encircle, a resource center for LGBTQ youth and their families in her community. She and her family wanted to volunteer there. She recalled the miracle that happened when she and her family took a risk to love people:

> What I hadn't really stopped to consider was that my brothers and sisters in the LGBTQ community might have something to offer me—that I might need them. As soon as my family walked in the door, we were welcomed, quite literally, with open arms. My children found other children to play with, and new friends offered us food and let us into their lives. I was struck by the sense of community and closeness I felt there and by how quickly this new circle of friends had opened up to us. I left Encircle that day not as the rescuer I had imagined myself to be but as the rescued.

A writerly friend of mine told me once to always state my agenda, and yes, I have an agenda here. Only, it isn't an agenda specific to any one ideology, political ideation, or philosophy. It is simply this: I want you to walk away with the guiding principles of grace, love, unity, and nonjudgment and become more like our Savior Jesus Christ in every aspect of your life. And I want to do the same. Holiness requires us to embody these principles—even in situations where there are people with whom we disagree. It sounds simple, but I know that it is not. For every time we've succeeded, there are scores of times we've failed. But I also don't want to discount the times we have chosen the love of Christ! Remembering what it feels like to choose Him gives us hope that we *will* be able to again. I hope we can love well time after time after time till it's harder to feel divided than united with our fellow man.

If we want to love like this, we have to build our lives in humility. We must have soft hearts, be teachable, be willing to change our minds, and get comfortable with the discomfort of trying to see things from another person's perspective. Humility is the soil in which love can grow.

In my quest to create a Zion-like experience for the people I walk this world with, I am trying to do the following: Assume the best in others. Allow others permission to be themselves while still standing by my firmly held beliefs. Like the good people of Quincy, reach out in love when I am needed—even if my beliefs are different. Make a space for anyone needing refuge. Every day, look for someone totally different from me and discover what about us is actually the same. See if I can love and find compassion even when I vehemently disagree. And, of course, I'm trying not to judge the judgers—or myself.

"A new commandment I give unto you, That ye love one another; as I have loved you, that ye also love one another."[88]

* * *

What do you want to be? These things? Others? What are the attributes that take a life away from the world and make it sacred? "If there is anything virtuous, lovely, of good report or

---

88 John 13:34.

praiseworthy,"[89] that is what I want to be. And I'm going to try. Every day.

> If Christ were to come today, He would know you.

If Christ were to come today, He would know you. Whether or not we are perfectly executing any of these attributes, we are doing the brave work of becoming holier for ourselves and, in so doing, are feeling the peace that comes with being like Him. We don't have to earn His love or devotion with our performance. His love for us is engraven on His hands and feet. His devotion in His side. We just have to choose Him. With bravery, step out of the crowd that doesn't know who just walked in. It's Christ. You know Him, and you are brave enough and holy enough to fall before Him, crying, "Master, Master, Master!"

---

89 A of F 1:13.

Chapter Eight

questions in one hand, faith in the other

"But behold, if ye will awake and arouse your faculties, even to an experiment upon my words, and exercise a particle of faith, yea, even if ye can no more than desire to believe, let this desire work in you, even until ye believe in a manner that ye can give place for a portion of my words."

—Alma 32:27

I love red nail polish. Think red balloons, fire engines, nails in the 1940s. Bold. My daughters beg me to try other colors, but no matter how long I take picking a color, I somehow find my way back to some version of red. I may have thinning hair, an expanding waistline, and new laugh lines every day, but I will have lovely nails! Amen!

One morning, after choosing my perfect shade of red at the salon, I was talking with Liv,[90] my nail technician. We were chatting about our lives, and she asked what I was working on.

I settled into my swiveling chair and leaned forward, ready to answer and engage in a meaningful conversation. I love talking about my work and getting other women's perspectives

90 Name has been changed.

on topics I'm writing about. I said, "I'm working on a chapter about the holiness found in asking questions and seeking understanding when you have questions regarding the gospel. I want to let women know that it is holy to wonder."

There was a long pause.

"Hmmmm," she said, her brows furrowing with honesty before she smoothed them out and said, "That's nice."

I heard her polite brush-off, but I was intrigued by the first part of her response and the brow furrow. "'Hmmm' what?" I asked.

"Oh, nothing!" She paused.

"No, I really want to know," I said. "What was your initial reaction of 'Hmm'?"

"It's just that I don't think of myself that way."

"What way?" I asked.

"As questioning. Or wondering. Or as anything but a confident daughter of God. I know I'm doing my best, I know who I am, and I don't have anything I wonder about the gospel. I really don't think I'd read a chapter about questions."

My initial reaction was surprise. Were there people in this world who didn't live daily, sometimes hourly, with questions running around in their thoughts? This gave way to a whole litany of emotional reactions within a couple of seconds. Following surprise, my reaction was to think (with a heap of condescension) that she was just young and naïve. My third reaction was to conclude that she was lying for the sake of appearances . . . Surely everyone has questions. EVERYONE. Right? I then reacted internally with resentment and envy. Why does she get to live in this peaceful state of non-questioning while my head is constantly spinning with wonder? How can she not have similar thoughts about all the questions that occupy my mind? My final reaction, the one I settled on as true, came as I looked into her beautiful eyes and sensed a soft and guileless goodness about her. This scriptural phrase about gifts of the Spirit from Doctrine and Covenants 46 came to mind: "To some it is given to *know*." I looked at her strong smile, and I believed her. She doesn't have questions. She just knows.

"Is that bad?" she asked. "Do you think I *should* have questions?"

I looked at her with awe. "No, Liv, that's not bad," I said. "That's a gift."

If you are like Liv, I say the same thing to you. Just as it is perfectly acceptable to have questions, it is also okay not to question. It's a gift of the Spirit. Some have one; some have the other. Neither gift is better or worse than the other. Neither qualifies or disqualifies you. If you find yourself free of questions, go ahead and skip a few pages. I'll meet you at the next chapter. If, on the other hand, you find yourself more like me, read on; the rest of the chapter is for us.

So you have some questions. Sister, let's get one thing out of the way right off the bat. You are *not* in a faith crisis. If you were, you wouldn't be reading a book about holiness. "Yeah, but . . . ," you might think and then, heart full of fear, rattle off a list of shocking questions to prove to me what a crisis you are in. You can't scare me with your questions. I stand by my assertion: you are not in a crisis of faith.

I have no idea where the term "faith crisis" came from, but I hate it. The first time I heard the expression, I was listening to someone explain their questions, many of which mirrored my own. In that moment, what I used to call curiosity, one of

my most distinc-
tive and beloved
traits, by the way,
now had a pallor
of darkness over
it. Suddenly, I
went from being
curious to being

> The only crisis of faith
> is the one that pleads
> indifference toward God.

in a *crisis*! Shame, fear, and turmoil surrounding questions I
had rose to the surface. To this day, I have to remind myself
that my inquisitive mind is part of my divine nature. I'm the
person who asks eighty-five questions on historical tours, who
reads as many books as she can, who always wants to know
more, including the details of God and my religion.

Telling yourself that you are in a crisis is only going to fill
you with shame, fear, and anxiety. The only crisis of faith is the
one that pleads indifference toward God. The one that says you
don't care whether He is there or not. If you were to tell me
you have questions but you really don't care about the answers
or don't care to draw closer to God, I will concede crisis. Everything else is just wonder, and wonder will always draw you
nearer to God, not farther from Him. Try this on for size. Say
aloud, "I am in a faith crisis." How do you feel? Anxious, up-
set, confused? Now, say this aloud: "I am full of wonder about
my faith." Feel better? Me too. The word *wonder* tells me I am
seeking. It allows me to be full of peace so the Spirit can be
present in my search for answers about the nature of God. It's
amazing how changing one word can open the shades covering
a darkened heart and allow the light to slide in and spread out.
Whether the word *wonder* works for you or not, find a positive
word that describes your state of mind. I like *wonder* because it

invokes a sense of awe. With this shift in perspective, the Holy Ghost can join you and will banish the darkness of fear in favor of the light of peace. There is nothing crisis-filled about a heart turned to heaven, about a child looking for her Father.

When we view our questions as a crisis, we naturally look for an end to the crisis. We think if we only had the answers, the crisis would be over. What a limiting and damning belief! Many of us are engaged in the work of looking for answers as a way out—a finish line. In his book *Letters to a Young Mormon*, Adam Miller writes that "work chained to outcome is misery."[91] The sooner those of us who are blessed with the gift of curiosity can accept that we will never be to the finish line of our questions in this life, the sooner we will be out of misery and the calmer and less afraid we will feel. God didn't send us here to learn something, then park it on a beach for the rest of our mortal lives. He sent us here as part of an eternal progression. Peace will come when we cultivate the expectation that the resolution of one question will result in another question. Heavenly Father says, "I will give unto the children of men line upon line, precept upon precept, here a little and there a little; and blessed are those who hearken unto my precepts, and lend an ear unto my counsel, for they shall learn wisdom; for unto him that receiveth I will give more."[92] There is always more to receive.

When we stand in judgment of our questions, we might label them doubts or call ourselves doubters. But we are not doubters! Doubt looks away; wonder looks toward.

There was a time when I sat across a table from my stake president, ready to pass over my temple recommend.

---

91 Adam Miller. *Letters to a Young Mormon*, 2nd edition [Deseret Book Company and Neal A. Maxwell Institute, 2018].
92 2 Nephi 28:30.

"Why are you giving this to me?" he asked. "Have you broken your covenants?"

"No!" I said. "But I have so many scary questions." Over several minutes, I allowed the questions and my stories to flow out of me.

He pushed my recommend back over the desk to me. "This is yours," he said. "Congratulations, you're a seeker. So am I. So was Joseph Smith."

Many outside our faith may call Joseph Smith's questioning of which religion to join and then joining none of them a crisis of faith. We call it the Restoration. We look at it as the event that began the restoration of the fulness of the gospel of Jesus Christ. To us, Joseph's "crisis" was a very good thing!

The beginnings of understanding and accepting my path as a seeker crept in. The holy life of a seeker involves learning to hold our questions and our faith at the same time in equanimity. We do this as we see questions and faith as equal in importance and let go of the temptation to label our questions as bad and our faith as good.

What you hold lovingly in one hand as a question will ultimately move to the other hand as faith. The act of questioning with a desire to draw closer to God is an investment in eternal progression and the matter that makes up your eventual faith.

Think of a truth you hold as knowledge, such as "Jesus is with me all the time." That truth was once a question: "Lord, are you still there?" The line between the question and the faith was work. If you never wondered with a question, you would never know. Don't be surprised when a question in one hand has become faith in the other; don't be alarmed when the hand left empty receives another question quickly. And don't be surprised if the questioning hand is holding many questions at the same time. This is what happens to seekers.

One phrase that repeats itself time and time again in my mind is "I don't know." What if we just added one little word to the end of that statement? I don't know . . . yet. The word *yet* is a faith word. It implies that while I might not know or understand right now, I believe I will find understanding some-day, and I commit to the path of inquiry till someday becomes today. The word *yet* ignites a spark of hope that sets the question on its journey to faith. I have had a lot of "I don't know yets" turn into "I knows." I offer these statements: I know Christ is with us all the time. I know God answers prayers through other people. I know the Book of Mormon was brought to us by divine communication between God and a young boy. All of these statements of "I know" were once my questions. "I don't know . . . yet" is exciting!

Even if you spend your whole life searching for answers to questions that are never fully satisfied within you, even if you die with your questions still held close to your heart, you can still live a life of faithful devotion as you look to God for the answers. At the "Be One" event commemorating the fortieth anniversary of the restoration of the priesthood to all people, regardless of race, the life of one such seeker was narrated with this beautiful passage,

> Jane Manning James was baptized as a young woman and led eight members of her family to Nauvoo. When they arrived, they were—rebuffed by some. Others received them as friends and fellow saints including the prophet Joseph Smith and his wife Emma. *Throughout*

> *her life Sister James pleaded to receive her temple blessings and she died at the age of 94 without them. But the light of her testimony did not wane, in fact, it grew brighter with time.* Near the end of her life she declared, "I want to say right here, that my faith in the gospel of Jesus Christ as taught by The Church of Jesus Christ of Latter-Day Saints is as strong today, nay, it is, if possible, stronger than it was the day I was first baptized."[93]

Most of us cannot imagine living a holy and exemplary life while never being allowed to receive the fulness of our temple blessings or any gospel blessings we might desire in this life. Sister James lived, hoping for something she would not ever see come to pass in mortality. The questions she probably had remained *while* she lived a valiant life. Hers were and are daunting questions, even today. Yet, her testimony did not wane. As I was watching the televised event (one of the most inspirational programs I have ever witnessed) with a stage full of my brothers and sisters of color, I wondered at what Jane would think of the continual progress being made in the Church.

Should Sister James have given up her faith when blessings she knew she was entitled to were never afforded her on this earth? She could have, and many would argue that she would have been justified in that decision. Instead, she epitomized the concept of holding faith and questions at the same time. She set her life apart as holy and dedicated to Christ both in her faith and in her questions.

I do not mean to diminish or trivialize the gravity of questions, especially questions as serious as those that arise from

---

93 *"Be One"* 37:15; emphasis added.

race or gender. My own questions were and are very serious to me, as are yours to you. Some of mine have moved from the hand of question to the hand of faith quickly; some have lived for many years in a place along the road from one hand to the other, and some may remain in the hand of questions for the whole of my mortal life. But in regard to my remaining questions, I hope they live in a place of hope, where one day I can say like Jane Manning James that "my faith is as strong, nay stronger" than ever, in spite of my unresolved questions. I am at peace with this possibility because I know life isn't linear—it's round. "Listen to the voice of the Lord your God, even Alpha and Omega, the beginning and the end, whose course is one eternal round, the same today as yesterday, and forever."[94] With this knowledge, I move forward without fear and with confidence. You can too!

> Let go of the expectation that we need to have all our answers right now, and embrace that our existence is about growth and development.

Let go of the expectation that we need to have all our answers right now, and embrace that our existence is about growth and development. We cannot grow once we know everything. We will always wonder. We will have questions. We

94 Doctrine and Covenants 35:1.

will have concerns. Perhaps even in the next life. As we accept this wonder as a beautiful part of our soul's growth, we become at peace with our path and better able to hear the whispering of the Holy Ghost.

I know your path as a seeker might scare people: your friends, family, people in your ward. Have patience with their fear, but don't allow their fear to make you feel less-than within yourself. They might have questions too, and their way of dealing with their questions might be different from yours, leading to perceived or real judgment on their part. They might not be seeking wonderers like we are. Look at your fearful loved ones without contention as I looked at my nail tech who didn't question. They might not understand your gift, but you can see the beauty in theirs. Remember, "to some it is given to *know*." Don't worry about their path. Focus on keeping your covenants and learning to walk the path of holding faith and questions together. God is not afraid of your questions. He and our Heavenly Mother and our Brother Jesus Christ are excited by them. They know that as you choose Them, your questions have the ability to make you more like Them, more godly, not less.

One Sunday, a friend[95] gave a talk in church that made this point: treat everyone as if they were an investigator, and everything they do becomes exciting. If an investigator to the gospel of Jesus Christ came to church and asked a controversial or scary question, we wouldn't be afraid or disappointed that they were asking. We would be excited that they were interested! We would dive in and seek to help them find the answers, providing much love and support. Yet, how many

95 Yes, you, Jake Carter, referencing Bradley D. Foster's talk, "It's Never Too Early, It's Never Too Late" from October 2015 General Conference.

times have you sat in judgment of someone asking a question, even if that someone was yourself? I have chided myself time after time for my wonder. If you find yourself relating, sister, stop! You and I are investigators of the gospel of Jesus Christ. We have taken His name upon us, but we are still learning. Treat yourself, your children, your family members, and your friends with the excitement that comes when you are turning toward Christ and wondering. Every investigative soul needs the support we give to brand-new investigators of the gospel.

Desire for further understanding is a gift! In her ground-breaking research, Dr. Carol Dweck discovered that people have one of two mind-sets: fixed mind-sets and growth mind-sets. People with fixed mind-sets believe that understanding and intelligence either are or are not inalterable. Those with growth mind-set, on the other hand, have "the understanding that abilities and intelligence can be developed."[96] She says this about growth mind-set: "When [people] believe they can get smarter, they understand that effort makes them stronger. Therefore, they put in extra time and effort, and that leads to higher achievement."[97]

When we believe that we should just know all things that relate to spirituality and religion, we are practicing a fixed mind-set. When we believe that a spiritual question can, through our faith, ultimately lead to an increase in spiritual intelligence, we are practicing a growth mind-set. Furthermore, it is suggested that as we adults cultivate the ability to look at our lives with growth mind-set, we teach our children to do the same. I can think of no greater gift than creating an environment in which

---

96 Carol S. Dweck. Definition of Growth Mindset, mindsetworks.com; accessed October 8, 2018.
97 Ibid.

my children see their own questions as tools to make them more faithful, more spiritually intelligent, more willing to use the Atonement to grow, and more connected to God.[98]

As we learn and grow, we develop an excitement about the intelligence we receive, and it's natural to want to share what we learn. Our fellow members of Christ's Church can be great discussion friends. Additionally, some of my best study companions are not of my religion, but they care about me and about my faith. They choose to philosophize with me in a spirit of love and a desire for spiritual growth. We might not agree on every point of doctrine, but I know they care about me and what I care about. It is, however, wise to look to be conscientious with the knowledge we have earned. Pray for discernment as you choose what and with whom you share, and allow the Spirit to be your guide. Often, when we are in a place of light and peace, our discernment is clear. We will know what is appropriate to share and with whom.

On the other hand, when we find ourselves in a place of fear, doubt, and confusion, we need to take care about who we talk openly with about our questions. Sharing the faith I have gained from asking important questions is something I love to do when the time is right; however there have been times when I have discovered information that has troubled me, and I've had to think carefully about who I should bring my concerns to. Luckily, I have most often taken these questions to the right places for help: the scriptures, prayer, personal revelation, leaders who operate under the power of

---

98 The Church offers an amazing resource for "Seeking Further Understanding from Divinely Appointed Sources" at https://www.lds.org/si/doctrinal-mastery/acquiring-spiritual-knowledge/seek-through-divine-sources?lang=eng; October 19, 2018.

the priesthood (both men and women), mentors, etc. This is the very work of faith!

The most important thing to remember is we should not take disconcerting questions to those vulnerable in testimony, to online forums, or to casual friends. Before sharing information, we should ask ourselves whether it is faith or fear motivating us to share. I would be devastated to think that a question I had, then went on to work through until it became faith, was shared with someone who never put in the work to turn the question I presented to them into faith, transforming my question into their doubt instead.

Additionally, another challenge with sharing our most disconcerting questions with the wrong people is that there are those who appear to be friends who have ulterior motives with our fragile questions and sacred learning. There are "friends" who are seeking to mock our path and those who would want us to fall away. They might not even be aware they are doing so. I have never felt as unsafely vulnerable as I have when I have inadvertently shared a question with someone who didn't have my soul's eternal progression as a priority in our discussion. Conversations like these have left me feeling alone, empty, and afraid. "Give not that which is holy unto the dogs, neither cast ye your pearls before swine, lest they trample them under their feet, and turn again and rend you."[99]

Don't let that make you feel lonely. As we discussed previously, you are not in your questions alone. We hide because we are afraid. But ultimately, thanks to the Atonement of Jesus Christ, there's nothing to be afraid of, to hide from. Information cannot separate us from the love of God. Nothing can.

---

99 3 Nephi 14:6.

Many of our questions originated because we were raised in a different time from what we live in now. In the past, we as individuals and even as a church, weren't as transparent as we could have been with information, leading to the inadvertent result of people feeling deceived. Transparency in companionship with the Spirit is important, essential even, and anything that appears as "hiding" isn't what we should do. Year after year, transparency increases. Speaking to CES teachers, Elder Ballard instructed that "you should be among the first, outside your students' families, to introduce authoritative sources on topics that may be less well-known or controversial so that your students will measure whatever they hear or read later against what you have already taught them."[100] Don't be afraid of teaching or learning with the Spirit as your companion. Our newfound ability to begin letting go of fear continues to create a healthier, holier environment in which our children can ask questions.

The Church has taken a major step forward in transparency with the publication of four books in a collective representative history of the Church. No Church-produced book before has sought to be as forthcoming and representative as *Saints Vol. 1: The Standard of Truth*. In my own study of this and other books addressing questions, I have found that my faith and ability to relate to our church's past has only increased in delving into challenging topics. If I were to have hidden my questions in fear instead of engaging in study, I never would have known this feeling of companionship with our pioneer forbearers.

What scary things have I found while researching? I found that our history is colorful. Whose isn't? It brings up

100 M. Russell Ballard. "The Opportunities and Responsibilities of CES Teachers in the 21st Century," February 26, 2016, Salt Lake Tabernacle.

a lot of emotions. Yet, our history combined with where we are today has the power to create a narrative more inclusive

> **A**sking our questions and then looking for and finding the answers . . . gives us an identity.

and more real to life than the white-washed, rose-colored-glasses, flannel-board stories of the past. I relate much more to the *real* people and *real* stories I am learning about than the caricatures and happily-ever-afters of my youth. In a Church history symposium celebrating the anniversary of the publication of *Daughters in My Kingdom*, Sister Julie B. Beck said, "We were given some research indicating that individuals who knew and understood Church history were much more likely to be faithful in their spiritual observance and that they tended to have a greater sense of identity in the church."[101] Asking our questions and then looking for and finding the answers—even when the answers are hard—gives us an identity. Seeing where we have been gives me hope for where we can eventually go.

There are times when things seem impossible, when our questions overwhelm us and we are left with but a tiny desire to believe among the overwhelming chaos of our confusion. We are like the father who brought his child before Christ to be healed of an unclean spirit. Mark 9:23 says, "Jesus said unto him, If thou canst believe, all things are possible to him

---

101 Julie B. Beck, "Preserving the Heritage of Latter-day Saint Women, 14:15." 2016 Church History Symposium.

that believeth. And straightway the father of the child cried out, and said with tears, Lord, I believe; help thou mine unbelief."[102] Is it not our faith that admits our unbelief? Is it not a desire to know Christ and to utilize the healing power of the Atonement that cries, "Help thou mine unbelief?"

Living the life of a seeker, you are going to be confused by apologists and critics. The apologists will tell you that everything you see as a concern or a question isn't true. They are going to tell you to have more faith. They are going to deny historical or scientific data. They will tell you that if your testimony were stronger, you wouldn't care about whatever it is you care about. The critics will tell you that your faith is ignorant and uninformed. They will condescendingly mock you for your belief and your devotion. These two extremes can cause confusion and frustration. But there is a voice in this middle place that trumps both the apologists and the critics, a voice that takes us out of our confusion and into a state of peace—it is the voice of the Savior.

Throughout time, those of us with inquisitive minds have sought the voice of the Savior over any outside sources as an answer to our questions. In his questions, Joseph Smith sought this voice out, followed it in the best way he knew, was confused by it, acted upon it, shared it, and ultimately died for it. There's not much difference between fourteen-year-old Joseph and people like us. We have the benefit of looking at Joseph's story over time, but the aftermath of Joseph's questions in a grove of trees continues to unfold. We will not live to see the end of his questions' story, but we see the effects of his faith in his mortal life and in our own. His is a story of

---

102 Mark 9:23–24.

questioning in faith and receiving answers. So too will our descendants look upon our stories not as those of doubt but as those of faith and wonder. They will see that we had serious questions, "nevertheless we knew in whom to trust."[103] Our lives will not be lives of crisis; they will be pilgrimages of faith and hope. In spite of everything, we will still choose God. This is not what the world would do. Ours will be lives set apart from the world. Our lives are holy in their questions.

---

103 2 Nephi 4:19.

Chapter Nine
finding holiness in change

"The only thing constant is change."

—Heraclitus

"The only thing constant is change," says the philosopher Heraclitus of Ephesus. Don't you want to punch him right in his pensive 535 BC face? I do, because he's right . . . and I hate it! I have to admit that it's the tiniest bit possible I am not writing from the best emotional place right now. The past thirty days of my life have been a master class in finding holiness in change. We decided to sell our well-loved family property on the Oregon Coast, my oldest started high school, my baby started full-time school, leaving me alone at home for seven hours a day for the first time in over fifteen years, we learned about some new and exciting (Don't I have a great attitude?) health challenges in our family, our longtime ward was split with only hours to prepare, and, to top it all off, I woke up this morning to what used to be a lovely mountain view out my bedroom window but is now a giant, permanent flagpole with an attached home developer's flag proudly proclaiming their presence! So yeah, I'm a little peeved at Heraclitus's obvious observation and ensuing cliché.

These changes are minor in the grand scheme of things, and I have certainly experienced much more significant life changes than those I mentioned, but no matter what you or I are experiencing, change feels disconcerting. New seasons leave us wondering what comes next, and we feel insecure as to our place in our own lives. In living a holy life, we have to learn to find holiness in places of discomfort, to choose faith over fear no matter what changes find us.

Ours is a living church. It will always change. But that's not my lesson to teach; it was Joseph Smith's, and it continues to be the current prophet's. The Doctrine and Covenants is comprised of evidence of our open heavens and continuing revelation, and each conference and even announcements in between offer the evidence for today. Since January 2018 when President Russel M. Nelson was called to be the prophet of The Church of Jesus Christ of Latter-day Saints, we have seen constant change. In a Mormon (Church of Jesus Christ of Latter-day Saint) Newsroom film, Sister Wendy Watson Nelson, our prophet's wife, gives us insight into the prophet's work of change: "I have seen him changing in the last ten months [since he became the prophet]. It is as though he has been unleashed. . . . He was foreordained to be the prophet of God on the earth today. . . . The restored gospel of Jesus Christ is a gospel of change. It's as simple as that. It's all about change. If we're not repenting, if we're not changing every day, then we're not true disciples of Jesus Christ."[104]

---

104 Wendy Watson Nelson on MormonNewsroom.org via Youtube. https://www.youtube.com/watch?v=rv48nEaU44Y&feature=youtu.be; accessed January 9, 2019.

In life, we can find ourselves attached to traditions. I'm guilty as charged. When our ward split, I gave myself a crygraine. (Crygraine: noun, a migraine headache that is the result of crying so hard that you can feel your heartbeat in your nostrils, and hearing loud noises makes you sick due to all the junk food you snarfed down whilst eating your feelings.) If holiness defined is a life set apart, then change in our church is the very thing that sets us apart, the very thing that makes us holy. We believe that the heavens aren't closed; that a prophet communicates with God today, and that next week, the way our church runs could be totally different than it is today. (With President Nelson at the helm, saying the Church could be run totally differently by next week isn't that much of an exaggeration! P.S. I wrote this before the October 2018 conference happened. We now have a two-hour Sunday block and are adopting a completely new focus for our worship. Point made.)

When we build our testimonies on things that might change, we can find ourselves reeling when that change inevitably happens. New ways of applying gospel principles to earthly life have challenged people to be adaptable from the foundation of the Church. What if instead of fearing change, we could learn to anticipate it as something to be expected? What if we could even be excited for changes within the Church?

One of the most fulfilling and exciting changes to the operation of the Church was the revelation President Spencer W. Kimball received in the upper rooms of the Salt Lake City temple on June 1, 1978. This revelation invited each of God's children, regardless of race, who chooses to live the commandments to be able to participate in temple covenants and ordinances and to have the authority to exercise the priesthood in all of its capacities. God revealed previously, "*He inviteth them all to come unto him and partake of his goodness; and he denieth none that come unto him, black and white, bond and free, male and female. . . . and all are alike unto God, both Jew and Gentile.*"[105] The thing is, this wasn't a "change of mind" that resulted in the revelation that became Official Declaration 2 in the Doctrine and Covenants. It was a change of people's hearts—a softening to the point that we were finally ready to receive a heavenly course correction that turned the operations of the Church to more closely align with God's will. *God never condoned the racism that existed* (and—let's be totally transparent—that in some situations still exists) within the culture of the Church.

If in May 1978 you would have asked an endowed member of the Church if they would be able to sit with their brothers and sisters of color in the celestial room of the temple the next month, most would have told you that no, they would not be allowed that blessing. But then, on June 8, 1978, it was announced that President Spencer W. Kimball had, "after extended meditation and prayer in the sacred rooms of the holy temple,"[106] received the revelation that all blessings of membership in Christ's Church would be extended to all people in the same way, regardless of color. For thousands of Saints of color—and the entire membership of the Church—this day changed the trajectory of their lives and ours and took the Church closer to the will of God.

Once members received the change, the leadership and membership of the Church moved forward, disavowing all racism that had previously been unintentionally and intentionally condoned. It is a process that continues today as we move toward a culturally inclusive world-wide sister and brotherhood. President Dallin H. Oaks, in the *Be One* event in June 2018,

105 2 Nephi 26:33.
106 Official Declaration 2.

said, "The reasons that had been given to try to explain the prior restrictions on members of African ancestry, even those previously voiced by revered church leaders, were promptly and publicly disavowed. . . . The Lord had spoken through His prophet and His church obeyed."[107]

The revelation came when we, as imperfect Church members, had become humble enough and were ready to be corrected. It was from this place of thousands of people begging, fasting, fighting, and praying for further insight that we were finally ready to understand the will of God through our prophet Spencer W. Kimball. We know of God's infinite love for each of His children. God never changed His mind. We changed our hearts. It is now our job, with this and other issues, to continue faithfully executing change and living closer to the people God wants us to be. Elder Oaks says, "As servants of God who have the knowledge and responsibilities of his great plan of salvation we should hasten to prepare our attitudes and our actions institutionally and personally to abandon all personal prejudices."[108]

And though some of us struggle with change, there are others right now praying to understand God's will, even praying for change in their

> It is now our job . . . to continue faithfully executing change and living closer to the people God wants us to be.

---

107 Be One event, Dallin H. Oaks talk.
108 Ibid.

own lives. Sister Carol F. McConkie reminds us that our "holiness is in the striving and the struggle to keep the commandments and to honor the covenants we have made with God."[109] For some, continuing faithfully is striving and struggle. If we want changes, if we have questions, it is my hope that we can find it in ourselves to stay in Church membership and be part of the prayers that turn the ship. What is God waiting to reveal to us? After all, "we believe all that God has revealed, all that He does now reveal, and we believe that He will yet reveal many great and important things pertaining to the Kingdom of God."[110] If we don't stay and ask, we might never see the revelations that will come as a result of thousands of us praying, pleading, and yearning. I agree with Elder Robert C. Gay of the Seventy when he said, "Whatever the price you must pay to trust Him is worth it."[111]

I know that for some it isn't easy to continue in Church membership. For many reasons, there are those who feel they can't remain. We don't judge these sisters and brothers. We don't pretend to understand their motivation or their testimony. Our paths are not their paths. We cannot presume to understand pain. Only Christ can do that.

For those who, in their questions, choose to stay, continue with your hopeful seeking for further revelation to come! As individuals, families, communities, and a church as a whole, we look to heaven with hope!

How thankful we should be that the heavens are open, that revelation is real, that God speaks to us today! His scriptures say:

109　Carol F. McConkie. "The Beauty of Holiness," *Ensign*, May 2017.
110　A of F 1:9.
111　Robert C. Gay. "Taking upon Ourselves the Name of Jesus Christ," *Ensign*. November 2018.

Doctrine and Covenants 121:26 "God shall give unto you knowledge by his Holy Spirit, yea, by the unspeakable gift of the Holy Ghost, that has not been revealed since the world was until now."

Daniel 2:28 "But there is a God in heaven that revealeth secrets."

Amos 3:7 "Surely the Lord God will do nothing, but he revealeth his secret unto his servants the prophets."

Doctrine and Covenants 88:63 "Draw near unto me and I will draw near unto you; seek me diligently and ye shall find me; ask, and ye shall receive; knock, and it shall be opened unto you."

3 Nephi 27:29 "Therefore, ask, and ye shall receive; knock, and it shall be opened unto you; for he that asketh, receiveth; and unto him that knocketh, it shall be opened."

JST Mark 9:45 "Seek unto my Father, and it shall be done in that very moment what ye shall ask, if ye ask in faith, believing that ye shall receive."

One of my Laurels and I recently had a talk about our need as adult women to lean on the youth of the Church. In a quickly changing world and church, it's exciting to be able to look to them for support. They are awesome and adaptable in ways that we could never dream of being. They teach us the ways of a modern world, how to have open minds, and that there is safety in pure-hearted seeking for truth. And yes, every time a new version of the iPhone is released, they teach me how to use it. (My young women also teach me about having fantastic eyebrows, which is a huge bonus.) If we asked our youth what they bring to the table (I know because I did ask them), this is what they would say: "The world has changed a lot in a short amount of time. During this time, women have become more independent and outspoken and a little less afraid. It's important to learn from new generations that it's okay to share what you're thinking and feeling rather than holding it all back. It's amazing to see something from a different perspective. It completely changes how you think about things. Especially when you've been seeing something the same way your entire life. Change is good."[112]

How thankful we are to be a gospel, a church, and a people of change. The person I am today is not the person I was years ago. The ever-changing circumstances in my life *required* me to change. I could have walked forward or backward, but I couldn't stay still.

Through Christ's Atonement, I chose to walk forward, and I have made changes that have taken me farther from the world and closer to Him. I have a long way to go. I'm guessing you feel that way too, but sis, look at how far we've come!

Practices within the Church will evolve through inspiration and revelation. Our own ideas and practices will come and go. Womanhood itself is an ever-shifting experience. Choosing to accept change rather than fight against it is a holy practice.

> How thankful we are to be a gospel, a church, and a people of change.

112 Jaylie Jackson, Pleasant Grove, Utah.

When Ruth Lybbert Renlund, prominent attorney and wife to Apostle Dale G. Renlund, was a twenty-five-year-old mother of one child, she was diagnosed with ovarian cancer. While she ached deeply, she eventually came to a place in which she was able to embrace change. Sister Renlund described her experience this way. "I always thought we'd have more children, so we grieved when we found out that we'd only have one child. Of course, adoption was an option, but because my health was uncertain, we weren't sure if I would be around to raise the child I had. I prayed for guidance, and at that point we knew our family was complete. I was impressed to go to law school and fulfill a deep-seated desire."[113] Having a child was holy, but when increasing their family size ceased to be an option, embracing change and practicing law was the holy choice for the Renlund family. When an unwanted change occurred, Sister Renlund fulfilled a deep-seated desire. She prayed, then used her agency to choose to spend her life in law, something she wanted to do!

In the past few weeks, I have watched one of my dearest friends, a sister of my heart who loves every bit of the life she leads, submit to holiness as she prepares to move to a new country for her husband's job. Every aspect of her life will be different. The language, her responsibilities, the culture, the safety of engaging in her community, schools for her children—everything. Due to the nature and location of the work, she will spend a lot of time alone with her children. She has spent her life building her family surrounded by grandparents, aunts and uncles, close friends, and lots of cousins for her children to grow up with. She is walking away from her tribe—the village that raised her, then helped raise her children—and walking into a new life.

---

113 "Just Call Me Ruth," *The Mormon Women Project,* May 12, 2010.

As we talk on the phone and send videos through a messaging app, I am amazed by her strength. While we talk, three of her kids run around the room and her new baby is snuggled to her chest. Through our exchanged messages, I can see the home she has created and all of the memories I have in that home. I don't want her to go. She talks to me about how sad she'll be to be in a place where her kids can't ride bikes around the neighborhood. She talks about leaving family and missing her nieces and nephews growing up. "Why didn't I marry an orthodontist?" she jokes with a sigh. She owns her sadness and nervousness, yet her overall message is the peace of submission and faith that God has a plan for her family. Most would feel sorry for themselves. (I know I would!) But not this sister of mine. She looks forward, knowing that God needs her to go. She is holy.

Governments may fall. People we love will die. Relationships may shift or end completely. Carefully constructed life plans might fall apart. A job we love may seem secure one day and be gone the next. We live in the rickety cart of an old-fashioned roller coaster that is our life.

In Heraclitus's mind, the only thing constant was change. And I've spent these pages explaining how he is right. But in a world defined by its ever-changing nature, there is one thing that will never change: the gospel and love of Jesus Christ—"For I am the Lord, I change not."[114] I cannot imagine living without this one solid truth. Jesus is our Savior; He died for us. He will not change. And that can give us courage.

Don't be afraid of change. I'm going to try not to be afraid either. I am going to go to the store for some cookies that I

---

114 Malachi 3:6.

will bring home to put on a pretty plate so it looks as if I made them myself, and then I'm going to gird up my loins and cross the street to attend my new ward's get-to-know-you party. I am going to prove to myself that the Church is still true on the other side of 900 West. I am going to try not to literally look behind me at the homes of my brothers and sisters who took care of me through an entire pregnancy of bed rest, the ones who officiated priesthood blessings for me when I needed them, the ones who challenged me with their different points of view, the ones who loved my children, the ones who have been my sisters and surrogate mothers, the ones who saw me and my family and who allowed me to serve them in my own humble and, many times, imperfect ways. No, I won't look back. I'm going to stand up tall, hold my plate of grocery-store cookies, reach out my hand to an autumn field full of strangers, and say, "Hi, I'm Christie. I'm your sister."

Chapter Ten
holiness in whole-ness

"Daughter, be of good comfort;
thy faith hath made thee whole."

—Matthew 9:22

Lately, I've become curious. (Well, that isn't exactly right; I've always been curious. Just ask any of my elementary school teachers, four of whom were rumored to have retired immediately following the year in which I was their student. Coincidence or complete exhaustion and near mental collapse from my never-ending litany of questions? You can be the judge on that one.) I was reading in Matthew 5:48: "Be ye therefore perfect, even as your Father which is in heaven is perfect." Naturally, I sigh a little whenever I read this verse. It's confusing. Why would Heavenly Father ask me to attain a state I am incapable of attaining in this life? As Elder Jeffrey R. Holland said in his brilliant (as always) talk "Be Ye Therefore Perfect—Eventually," "Such celestial goals seem beyond our reach. Yet surely the Lord would never give us a commandment He knew we could not keep."[115] As I was reading, I saw something I've never noticed before in this scripture. It was

<hr>

115 Jeffrey R. Holland. "Be Ye Therefore Perfect—Eventually," *Ensign*. November 2017.

a little tiny b before the word *perfect*, suggesting a footnote. Being a footnote addict, I looked it up and found the most amazing thing. In the King James translation of the Bible, the word that was translated into *perfect* actually has an alternate translation that derives from Greek. This Greek translation takes the word *perfect* and replaces it with the word *complete*.

Shut the front door! (That is my Latter-day Saint exclamation of excitement!) What if the search for perfection, to be like God, has actually always been an invitation to be *complete* . . . to be whole?

Read it again this way: "Be ye therefore *complete*, even as I am *complete*." Am I the only one breathing the hugest sigh of relief over this? The word *complete* feels much more eventually attainable to me than our modern-day interpretation of the word *perfect*. Heavenly Father wants us to be complete. He wants us to be whole.

A further exploration of the footnotes we cross-reference for context leads us to another verse in Leviticus 19:2: "*Ye shall be holy: for I the Lord your God am holy.*" This cross-referenced scripture suggests to me that our quest for perfection/completeness/wholeness is really a quest for holiness. In order to live wholly, we must seek the holy. What does it mean for a woman of Christ's Church to live wholly?

There's a lot of talk these days about wholeness or whole living, and it's an important topic. When we hear the word *wholeness*, a concept of balance of the body, mind, and spirit is what we usually envision. This balance is essential to healthy living. So essential, in fact, that I dedicated an entire chapter in my first book to the type of wholeness found through balance of the body, mind, and spirit by implementing good habits of living in these three categories. [116] With enthusiasm, I recommend this kind of balance! It is important to work on our bodies, minds, and spirits in practical ways (i.e. healthy eating, exercise, learning, study, meditation, prayer).

These actions set us up for a healthy lifestyle. However, living wholly in practice is not of itself holy. We have to believe it too. A whole woman is one who embraces every part of what it means to be a woman. We need to think more about womanhood and our divine nature as women. When we rebuff any part of our womanhood or value it as "less than" simply because it is feminine, we are diminishing ourselves, and this makes it impossible to achieve this state of completeness we seek.

> A whole woman is one who embraces every part of what it means to be a woman.

When Joseph Smith saw the Father and the Son, he provided us with the knowledge of the characteristics we can expect our Mother in Heaven to possess: a body of flesh and blood, a voice, emotion, concern for us, etc. He taught of Their characteristics and our similarities to Them often. Then in 1909, the First Presidency taught us over the pulpit that "all men and women are in the similitude of the universal

---

116 Christie Gardiner. *You are the Mother Your Children Need,* Chapter 6, "Caring for your Body, Mind and Spirit."

Father and Mother, and are literally the sons and daughters of Deity."[117]

"The Family: A Proclamation to the World" seeks to differentiate gender in men from that in women while not putting one above the other. It says, "All human beings—male and female—are created in the image of God. Each is a beloved spirit son or daughter of heavenly parents, and, as such, each has a divine nature and destiny. Gender is an essential characteristic of individual premortal, mortal, and eternal identity and purpose."[118]

Our gender as women is an "essential characteristic" of our eventual godhood. "So God created man in his own image, in the image of God created he him; male and female created he them."[119] We were created in the image of our Mother in Heaven.[120] Our bodies are like Her body, and the things that make us women aren't uncouth or shocking. Just as a male body is sacred and amazing, so too are our female bodies. Every part we as women have on earth, She has in heaven: breasts, hips, a womb, and every other part of a reproductive system. The doctrine of The Church of Jesus Christ is clear on gender and actually quite unique. Learning to accept our bodies and appreciate every part and function of them as holy, sacred, and beautiful can help us feel more comfortable in our divine female identities.

As women, we are seeking to be complete, even as our Mother in Heaven is complete. While scriptural accounts do not

---

117 "The Origin of Man," *Improvement Era* 13, no. 1 (November 1909): 78, and lds.org Gospel topic essay, "Mother in Heaven." Accessed September 18, 2018.
118 *Ensign*. November 2010.
119 Genesis 1:27.
120 Seminary/Institute Question Answer Resources. https://www.lds.org/si/questions/mother-in-heaven?lang=eng; accessed October 25, 2018.

give us a lot of information about the nature of our Heavenly Mother, we can learn about Her characteristics from modern-day prophets and leaders through study, prayer, personal revelation, meditation, and common sense. Additionally, studying scriptural accounts of Her daughters gives us examples of the characteristics we as women seeking to be whole and holy can strive to attain.

The story of Queen Esther comes from chapter 4 of the book of Esther in the Old Testament. Esther was a Jewish orphan who was adopted and raised by her cousin Mordecai. Through a series of events, all of which had to perfectly align, Esther took up her divine calling to become queen. During her reign, an evil anti-Semite named Haman formulated a plan to massacre the Jews. Esther then asked for prayers and fasting as she attempted to go forward with an idea to save the Jewish people. Mordecai said to her, "And who knoweth whether thou art come to the kingdom for such a time as this?"[121] stating his belief that God put her in the exact place at the exact time to save her people, which, as we know, she goes on to do.

The woman with the issue of blood[122] did everything she could for twelve years to be relieved of her ailment. She spent all the money she had and went to every doctor in an attempt to get well, only to be made worse. Finally, she heard about Jesus, and with faith as the only thing she had left, she decided to seek Him out in a crowded place among a multitude of people. Somehow, after all she had suffered, she believed that if she could but touch Christ's robe, she would be made whole. She did, and she was. Upon this interaction, Christ stopped and asked His disciples who had touched Him. The

---

121 Verse 14.
122 Matthew 9, Mark 5, and Luke 8.

disciples pointed out the crowd and said that any number of people could have touched Him. But Christ knew that it was an intentional act, as he perceived that a portion of strength had left Him. The woman fell at His feet and admitted that it was she who had touched Him and then proceeded to tell Him her story. With compassion, Jesus told her that her faith had made her whole. The woman with the issue of blood was made whole through her faith, which was not in the act of touching the robe alone but in the many expressions of faith in the twelve years that proceeded her miraculous healing. Each prayer, each doctor's visit, each time she tried and failed yet still persisted to be made well was a sign of faith in her eventual healing. She lived a holy life in such a way that when she heard of the Savior, she knew who He was and found Him. Her faith made her whole and holy.

We love to read Proverbs 31:10: "Who can find a virtuous woman? for her price is far above rubies," but have you ever read verses 11–28? In these verses, we read that the virtuous woman has these qualities:

Is trusted by her husband (verse 11).

Does good deeds on behalf of her husband (verse 12).

Looks for wool and flax to work willingly with her hands and separate for future spinning of yarn (verse 13).

She brings food into the home—is a literal breadwinner (verse 14).

Wakes up early to feed her children and employees (verse 15).

Buys property (verse 16).

Plants a vineyard (verse 16).

Girdeth her loins with strength and strengtheneth her arms—physical and spiritual exercise (verse 17).

Works into the night on work that she perceives is good (verse 18).

Spins yarn (verse 19).

Serves and gives to the poor (verse 20).

Clothes her household in winter apparel (verse 21).

Makes herself nice clothes (verse 22).

Has a well-known husband (verse 23).

Sells linen and clothing to local stores (verse 24).

Clothes herself with strength and honor—spiritual development (verse 25).

Is kind and wise in her words (verse 26).

Keeps busy overseeing household work (verse 27).

Is called blessed and praised by her family (verse 28).

Proverbs 31:10 is often used to suggest sexual or moral purity, but as we can see from a closer look at the surrounding scriptures, we are actually being shown a whole list of character traits this virtuous woman possesses. And to tell you the truth, the virtuous woman is kind of giving me an inferiority complex. I look at this list of virtues, and while I might see an overachiever, I do not see weakness. I see strength, power, and holiness in the wholeness of womanhood.

Esther, the virtuous woman, Ruth, Eunice, certain women, Mary the Mother of Jesus, the woman with the issue of blood—

examples of Heavenly Mother-like strength saturate the scriptures. Much of the cultural messaging of the world tells women they must be weak and subservient, but tell me which of these scriptural women is weak? Which of these is subservient? We, both women and men, are told to be meek, but as my friend Holly loves to say, "Meekness isn't weakness." Meekness is "godfearing, righteous, humble, teachable, and patient under suffering."[123] Meekness is whole.

There is not and has never been one right way to be a woman. A whole and holy woman might be loud and forceful or soft and sweet. She might work either inside or outside of the home. She can choose any political persuasion. She might love to cook, clean, and sew, and she might not. But no matter her personality or life choices, she finds strength in knowing who she is, why she is here, and where she is going. She knows she is an important part in the family of God, a daughter of Heavenly Parents who love her. As you explore the myriad ways to express the person you are, remember Marianne Williamson's words: as a woman, "your playing small does not serve

> No matter [a whole and holy woman's] personality or life choices, she finds strength in knowing who she is, why she is here, and where she is going.

---

123   Guide to the Scriptures. "Meek," "Meekness"; accessed at lds.org on September 18, 2018.

the world."[124] In order to embrace our divine femininity, we have to let go of the cultural and societal stereotypes of what it means to be a woman. We can neither put our divine femininity on a pedestal, nor value it beneath the characteristics of the divine masculinity.

Feminine is a powerful word, not a small one. You have a feminine voice and feminine characteristics. This matters. The kind of subservience that strips us of our agency was never God's plan. Submitting to a practice, ideology, whim, or demand of another person without our own conviction of doing so is not what it means to be a woman. Any man who would seek to take away our agency in any way is not acting in accordance with God's plan for His children or the doctrine of the Church. President Hinckley said, "Under the plan of heaven, the husband and the wife walk side by side as companions, neither one ahead of the other, but a daughter of God and a son of God walking side by side."[125]

Likewise, using stereotypical behaviors of our gender to manipulate a man to submit is not something we as women who recognize and appreciate the divinity of both genders should ever do. (I'm guilty of this. I have cried to get out of a speeding ticket. I know, gross, right? I am not proud of it.) We have to be aware of the ways we stereotype the men around us and don't allow them to experience being whole men. It is sad when boys are told not to cry, as if the Savior Himself did not weep with Mary and Martha when Lazarus

124 *A Return to Love: Reflections on the Principles of a Course in Miracles*, [Harper Collins, 1992], Chapter 7, Section 3, 190–191.
125 Gordon B. Hinckley. Fireside, Buenos Aires, Argentina, 12 November 1996; referenced on lds.org, "Latter-day Counsel: Selections from Addresses of President Gordon B. Hinckley."

died[126] or cry over the city of Jerusalem.[127] It similarly discourages me when the strength of men is diminished.

In our workplaces, homes, Church settings, and every other aspect of our lives, we need to be women who are strong enough to allow men to be whole men, and we need to surround ourselves with men who are strong enough to allow women to be whole women. "Nevertheless neither is the man without the woman, neither the woman without the man, in the Lord."[128]

It is time for us all to separate old stereotypical ideals from the never-changing, divine characteristics of gender. Some would say there are not divinely appointed differences in gender, but as women in Christ, we know there most certainly are! Denying differences in gender inhibits ourselves and others from experiencing a fulness of Their creation. We don't seek to be exactly like our brothers; rather, we seek to embrace our femininity (whatever it means to us) and acknowledge the differences as equal in import and necessity.

We must strip ourselves bare of the cultural messaging of the world. We are entitled to "choose for [ourselves]"[129] the way we will live our lives. Just like the virtuous woman, we can take on the many different responsibilities we put into our lives and execute them with the touch of divine feminine. As you, with strength in your whole womanhood, take up the mantle of whom God made you to be, you will find a life set apart in your work and a connection to heaven

---

126 John 11:35.

127 Luke 19.

128 1 Corinthians 11:11.

129 Moses 3:17 "Choose for thyself."

purer than ever before. This is where holiness is found. You were never meant to be small. You were meant to be whole. You were meant to be you.

After all that we can do in this life to live as whole women, it will be by the grace of our Savior and His Atonement that we will be saved.[130] I can't wait to fall, not only in my weakness but also in my womanly strength, at the feet of my Savior. To place my hands upon His nail-scarred feet and, with the love of a sister, thank Him for His endless grace that has made me whole.

---

130 2 Nephi 25:23.

Chapter Eleven
creating home-centered, church-supported holiness

"Part of the Lord's current sharing of knowledge relates to accelerating His pouring out eternal truth on the heads and into the hearts of His people. He has made clear that the daughters of Heavenly Father will play a primary role in that miraculous acceleration."[131]

—Henry B. Eyring

I'd heard the rumors of two-hour church for years. I didn't pay much attention to them. I thought it was about as likely as soda machines in ward-house kitchens. And then came along President Nelson with the inspiration that "it is time for a home-centered church, supported by what takes place inside our branch, ward, and stake buildings."[132] I welcomed the announcement with joy and relief! Serving in the Church brings me great satisfaction and fulfillment, yet my Sundays were overwhelmingly burdened by the administrative side of my calling. Meetings seemed to consume my Sabbath. I remember sitting in tears after a particularly intense week with

131 "Women and Gospel Learning in the Home," *Ensign*, November 2018.
132 Russell M. Nelson. "Opening Remarks," *Ensign*, November 2018.

my calling's administrative responsibilities. I cried to a friend and wondered if my children were being lost in the work of my calling (which I loved, by the way). My friend sent me a text that said, "Don't worry, Dallin H. Oaks says help is on the way!" I assumed it was one of those things she'd heard from a friend who'd heard it from a friend. But I believed and hoped just enough to look it up. And I found the source! Two months before the announcement, Elder Oaks said, "We have spent many hours talking about how we can simplify our Church programs to perform their essential function for a wide variety of family circumstances. Now, I am pleased to tell you that some help is on the way and more is under discussion."[133]

It just felt right. We weren't being offered a "free pass," and it wasn't less church that was being implemented. What we were being offered was a complete paradigm shift. We have been given an invitation to return the focus of our worship from a correlated experience to an experience in which each individual and family in the home can learn from the scriptures and manuals combined, as well as personally tailored revelation. President Nelson explained the change by noting, "We are each responsible for our individual spiritual growth. And scriptures make it clear that parents have the primary responsibility to teach the doctrine to their children."[134]

Some of us have been doing this for years. Most of us are just getting our feet wet in the depth and breadth of

---

133 Dallin H. Oaks. Question and Answer Session, Los Angeles, California, August 24, 2018.
https://www.lds.org/church/news/president-oaks-answers-tough-questions-from-rising-generation-raising-next generation?lang=eng: accessed October 15, 2018.
134 Russell M. Nelson. "Opening Remarks," *Ensign*, November 2018.

individual and family study outside of church. It's exciting! It is as if we have been given permission to do the work that somewhere deep inside of us we have always known is ours.

As my friends and I have talked about the first steps we've taken in implementing this new plan, I've been impressed and inspired by the variety of ways my friends are undertaking this teaching in their homes and with their families. I love brainstorming and learning what has worked and what hasn't for my friends and for my own family. Creative, ingenious, and inspired ideas are coming together in our talks, and we are each taking them to the Lord and making them our own. One family I know has started having their family night on Thursdays, following Elder Quentin L. Cook's revealing the position of the Church that "time spent in home evening, gospel study and activities for individuals and families may be scheduled according to their individual circumstances."[135]

It's fun to chat with our friends about their ideas and methods, but there are times when we are tempted to wonder what our neighbors are doing in a not-so-healthy way—in judgment. Perhaps we judge the way our neighbors are interpreting this new charge, or maybe we see the great things our neighbors are doing and are tempted to judge ourselves. Sister, listen to Elder Uchtdorf and "*Stop It*!"[136] In conference it was said, and is repeated in the *Come, Follow Me—For Individuals and Families* manual, that each of us will structure our home study in different ways. There isn't a wrong or a right way to teach the gospel, simply a right way for your family. The most effective ways to accomplish a home-centered church for our

---

135 Quentin L. Cook. "Deep and Lasting Conversion to Heavenly Father and the Lord Jesus Christ," *Ensign*, November 2018.
136 Dieter F. Uchtdorf. "The Merciful Shall Obtain Mercy," *Ensign*, May 2012.

own families will be shown to us through personal revelation. What's right for me and my family might not be what's right for you and yours. And vice versa.

In the short time since we have begun, I've been excited to see the change in our family, and I look forward to the sacred environment our family will help each other create inside our home. We've been told that our homes can be as sacred as a temple. The Bible Dictionary says that temples are "a place where the Lord may come, it is the most holy of any place of worship on the earth." But it goes on to say this: "Only the home can compare with the temple in sacredness."[137] Only the *home*. Not the ward building, not the stake center. The *home*.

As we embark on this noble effort, can I make an observation? There are those around us, maybe even ourselves, to whom this announcement came with some worries. Single-parent families, new members, single adults, widows and widowers, people new to our neighborhoods, part-member families, empty nesters, and others might all experience some loneliness as they think about losing a precious hour of association with their brothers and sisters each week. For this reason, I love that we are encouraged to have small-group studies. As explained by Elder Cook, "It would be completely appropriate . . . to gather in groups outside the normal Sunday worship services to enjoy gospel sociality and be strengthened by studying together the home-centered, Church-supported resource. This would be accomplished informally by those who so desire." Small groups gathered together to learn and grow in the gospel are powerful. Not having studied the Book of Mormon as much as I would have liked in my youth, I was thrilled to be a part of a scripture-study group in my twenties

---

137   Bible   Dictionary.   "Temple."   https://www.lds.org/scriptures/bd temple?lang=eng&letter=T; accessed October 15, 2018.

in which I first clearly understood the time line of the Book of Mormon. It was an important time for me. In consonance with provided materials and the scriptures, small-group study can be an important part of our gospel learning.

Yes, it is all very exciting. Can I admit that it's scary too? I look at salvation—both mine and the salvation of those over whom I have stewardship—as the ultimate goal. Suddenly, the ability for any of us to accomplish this "ultimate goal" feels as if it is resting on me. It feels very serious. It's heavy. Every time I turn on the news and see the events of the earth, I feel keenly the importance of rooting ourselves and our families in the gospel of Jesus Christ.

But how is it possible for me to root my family in the gospel with the scourges of today's society all around me? At the women's general session in 2018, President Eyring said, "Part of the Lord's current sharing of knowledge relates to accelerating His pouring out eternal truth on the heads and into the hearts of His people. He has made clear that the daughters of Heavenly Father will play a primary role in that miraculous acceleration."[138] Right away, I sensed the importance of my holy role and went to work studying with a worried heart in an effort to understand how to take this new responsibility upon myself. For many days following the conference, part of his message looped continually through my mind: "The daughters of Heavenly Father will play a primary role." *But I'm not a scriptorian*, I kept thinking. *I aspire to be a gospel scholar, but it seems the more I study, the more I know what I don't know. How do I do this?* With these questions, I sought to find women in the scriptures who had been instrumental in the gospel teaching of their children. I came first upon the mothers of the stripling

138 "Women and Gospel Learning in the Home," November 2018.

warriors, whose sons were so empowered by their examples that no trace of doubt was found in them in spite of perilous circumstances.

I then read of Mary, Elisabeth, Hannah, Sarah, Lucy Mack Smith: all valiant mothers who also taught the gospel. One scriptural mother stuck out to me personally: Eunice, the mother of Timothy.

In the New Testament, Timothy was a young man with what the Apostle Paul called "unfeigned faith."[139] Paul points out that Timothy's precious faith "dwelt first in thy grandmother Lois, and thy mother Eunice."[140] Paul teaches Timothy of sin and warns him of the world in the last days but tells him not to be afraid before giving him courage with these words: "Con-

> The foundation of testimony given to Timothy by his mother and grandmother led him to believe the gospel when he met the Apostle Paul.

tinue thou in the things which thou hast learned and hast been assured of, knowing of whom thou hast learned them; and that from a child thou hast known the holy scriptures, which are able to make thee wise unto salvation through faith which is in

---

139 2 Timothy 1:5.
140 Ibid.

Christ Jesus."[141] Paul comforts Timothy by reminding him that he learned the scriptures and was assured of the gospel from the time he was a child at the feet of his mother. The foundation of testimony given to Timothy by his mother and grandmother led him to believe the gospel when he met the Apostle Paul. Although still in his youth, Timothy went on to help establish the Church and became an influential leader and follower of Christ. I have a love and appreciation for Eunice, the mother who not only taught the scriptures but also provided an environment in which Timothy was able to cultivate an honest and pure faith—the foundation of his ministry. I want to be like her. I want to create an environment for my children to learn the scriptures and a home in which they are free to find a faith unfeigned.

It's what I want for my children, but it scares me to death. I do, however, have one thing working in my favor: an internal commitment to keep showing up. If I don't know the gospel well enough now, I have to say, "Oh well!" There is nothing I can do about the past. From this point on, my family and I will learn what we need to learn together. In my "primary role," I will lead them with humility and an honest desire to learn.

My parents were imperfect parents (as 100 percent of parents are). Yet I learned my most cherished lessons about the gospel from my mother in non-conventional ways in our home, supplemented by weeks I spent in the summers with my father and stepmother. The two households in which I grew up couldn't have been more different in their parenting styles or approaches, but in both homes, I knew they loved the Lord, and they always turned to Him for support. They

---

141 2 Timothy 3:14.

weren't perfect. I had a less-than-ideal upbringing. Yet, for whatever each of them lacked, I am so thankful that their combined imperfect efforts somehow created an environment in which I was able to build a solid testimony that has sustained me to this point in my life. That is Christ's grace.

The scriptures don't tell us much about Eunice's life. They do, however, mention a household in which one parent was Jewish and one parent was Greek, likely presenting some challenges in different cultural upbringings. Additionally, although we don't know what happened to Timothy's scripturally unnamed father, it's noted that Eunice's mother, Lois, was influential in Timothy's life, suggesting his grandmother played an important role in his childhood. As a final clue to the challenges in Timothy's upbringing, the scriptures document the perilous times in which Eunice raised Timothy. God isn't asking us to be perfect mothers or expecting us to be in perfect circumstances. In fact, He probably won't prevent our difficulties. He is just asking us to show up, no matter our circumstances. Even in adversity and imperfection, we, like Eunice, can teach our children and give them experiences that will help them shape their testimonies. It's in our nature to nurture, a nature that came from our Mother in Heaven.[142]

And what if our children don't choose Christ's Church? Sister, it isn't over yet. Lucy Mack Smith had a son who wasn't sure about religion. That must have been nerve-wracking for her, but he'd learned the gospel from his committed parents, and this foundation of home-centered study ultimately led Joseph Smith to find a better way for his family and all of us. Don't be afraid. We are in the middle of an eternal life. You don't know

142 "Mother in Heaven," Gospel Essay; https://www.lds.org/topics/mother-in-heaven?lang=eng: accessed October 15. 2018.

the end of the story. No matter what the confusion of a mortal life leads our children to choose for now, they can always look to our examples without questioning what we know to be true and what we practice. Whatever our individual situations happen to be, in spite of mistakes we make or imperfections we have, we are capable of being the mothers our children need! (Yes, I will say it forever: you are the mother your children need![143]) Don't be afraid. Like the stripling warriors, our children will not doubt that "their mothers knew it."[144]

We are the trailblazers for this new way of approaching learning and living the gospel! It's exciting, terrifying, humbling, and confidence promoting. As we blaze the trails for our daughters in the methods of home-centered, Church-supported coming unto Christ, may we take courage in the women who have come before us: the stripling warrior mothers, Lucy Mack Smith, Lois, Eunice, Hannah, Sarah, Elisabeth, and Mary. Our Heavenly Father trusted each of these women to imperfectly but faithfully light the way for their children in lives set apart for sacred purposes—just as He trusts us.

The promise Joseph Smith offered to sisters of the Relief Society applies to us as women seeking to create holiness in our homes through a home-centered Church. He said, "You are now placed in a situation where you can act according to those sympathies which God has planted in your bosoms. If you live up to these principles how great and glorious!—if you live up to your privilege, the angels cannot be restrained from being your

---

143 Christie Gardiner. *You Are the Mother Your Children Need: Believing in Your God-Given Gifts, Talents, and Abilities* [Covenant Communications Inc., 2017].
144 Alma 56:48.

associates. . . . If you will be pure, nothing can hinder."[145] With purity of heart, we go forward in faith, with angels at our sides, to a higher and holier time of learning in our lives and the lives of those we love most.

---

145 Joseph Smith. *Joseph Smith Papers*, discourse, 28 April 1842, as reported by Eliza R. Snow.

Chapter Twelve
holy relationships

"Let us relish life as we live it, find joy in the journey, and share our love with friends and family. One day each of us will run out of tomorrows."[146]

—Thomas S. Monson

On the afternoon of June 13, 2003, I held a brand-new baby in my arms. My first. A daughter. We named her Hailey Jane. My mom, grandma, and aunts had just arrived, and the room was abuzz with the chatter of the women in my life. I was nervous that they, these seasoned women, were watching me hold my baby. I was worried I wasn't doing it right. My grandma stepped close to me, put a comforting hand on my shoulder, then scooped my little six-pound peanut out of my arms and pulled the baby to her breast. I saw past the silver hair to the young mother my Gram had once been. She got close to me in my hospital bed and, looking at my baby, said, "Isn't it amazing? This little baby was just in heaven with my mother. I know my mother was helping get her ready to come to our family, and now, here she is, in our arms." I took comfort thinking of the

146 "Finding Joy in the Journey," *Ensign*, November 2008.

possibility of my great-grandmother's role in this life event as I watched Gram rock the baby, counting tiny fingers and whispering in my daughter's perfect ears.

I had no idea that blissful day that two months later, my mother, aunts, grandmother, and I would be in the hospital together again. This time, all of us surrounded Gram in her hospital bed. I held her hand and watched my strong mother whispering in her own mother's perfect ears—sweet words of gratitude about what an amazing mother she'd been. My aunts sat on the other side of the bed, and the four of us witnessed the labored breathing of our matriarch slow and eventually stop, sending—much too soon—this beloved woman from earth with us to heaven and the arms of our family waiting on the other side.

Four years later, I was again in labor. My second baby. Another daughter. I labored through the night and thought of this little spirit about to join my family. I remembered that day in 2003 with my first baby, and Gram's words came back to me. I pictured her standing nearby as my contractions came closer together. I swear I could almost hear her whispering to me, "Isn't it amazing? My mother helped Hailey from premortal life to earth, and this time, it's me. I'm with your daughter right now." I took comfort thinking of her helping my daughter get ready to come to our family, my beautiful daughter who would look like my grandmother and even be named for her, Elisabeth Suzanne.

I imagined the same heavenly pep talk when in the surgical room to deliver my son via cesarean section. When Christian Hansen was born, I knew I had heavenly help from both my grandmother and my husband's grandmother.

Birth and death are among the most holy of relational moments in this life. Life's big moments can be bonding, but the ability to find holiness in those moments comes because of the foundational relationships we develop with people close to us before the moment of significance. Holy moments of significance with the people we love are built upon thousands of everyday interactions.

Some people collect things; I collect people. Once we're friends, you'll be in my heart forever. I love building relationships, and I treasure each one. As I've poured my heart into the study of holiness, I've found it to be interesting that the most holy things in our lives are the things we get to keep when we leave this earthly life. Relationships are one of those things. In Doctrine and Covenants 130:2, we read that the "same sociality which exists among us here will exist among us there, only it will be coupled with eternal glory, which glory we do not now enjoy."

Looking over the holiest moments in the last seven days, they are moments shared with my people.

A week ago, I hosted a house full of teenagers (which I do every Friday): my daughter and her friends, who, let's be honest, were there for the food. Hot dogs and Doritos can be holy! Listening to them talk about their struggles and their hopes, hearing their laughter, dishing out unsolicited advice—it felt sacred in our house that Friday. If you have a teenager, send them over on Fridays. Tell them there's free food.

A few days ago, I screamed at my son. We were late for karate, and he couldn't find his belt. I yelled and yelled till we both got in the car and buckled up. I heard his little sniffles for the entire fifteen-minute drive. When we got to the studio,

I watched him hang his head as he walked through the door. I had forty-five minutes to do some pretty serious repenting. We drove home, and I went to his side of the car, opened the door, and, before he could jump

> The forgiveness of a child is a tender holiness.

out, took his little face in my hands, looked him in the eyes, which had begun to tear up again, and said, "I'm so sorry, son. Mommy made a mistake in yelling at you. You just needed someone to help you find your belt, and instead, Mommy yelled. I am so sorry I did that. I hope when you are ready, you will forgive me." He hopped down and ran into the house, yelling, "I forgive you, Mom." I knew I was really forgiven that night when I went to go to sleep and he'd put a giant plastic spider on my pillow. Practical jokes are how he says, "I love you." The forgiveness of a child is a tender holiness.

On Tuesday, my daughter didn't know I was watching her through the blinds in our family room. She was in the back-yard, and the honey locust trees were sighing and swaying in the wind. She had been working so hard on her tumbling skills, and I watched her fall over and over as she tried to land some sort of trick. As a momma, I wanted to run out there and scoop her up off the grass when she took a particularly hard fall. But I didn't. I let her fall and get back up. Over and over. A few minutes later, she stuck the landing. She threw her ponytail back and raised her arms in triumph, saying, "Yes! Yes! Yes!" to the sky, not knowing anyone was watching her at all. Her triumph was holy.

Wednesday, the Relief Society president of the ward from which I was just split and I were driving opposite directions.

She saw me pulling up to my house and pulled her car over to the side of the road. Likewise, I stopped my car and threw it into park right there in the middle of the driveway. Both of us left our driver's side doors open and met on the sidewalk in a long and tight embrace. "I love you," we both said. "This is hard," we both said. Then she got in her car and drove on, and I pulled into my driveway. Sisterhood is deep enough and holy enough to break your heart.

Yesterday, I held my baby niece, just hours old and, oh, so tiny. I looked at her mom and dad—my brother—and was so full of love for them. It's been a road for my brother and me. Seeing him as a happy dad to a baby girl fills my heart with so much love and joy and redemption . . . I could burst. It was holy.

Tonight, I sat with my nephews in a stairwell and talked about holiness. I meant to ask them one quick question about their opinions on a specific aspect of covenants and ordinances. It turned into an hour-long conversation in which the three of us sat together sharing sacred time. I held these two boys when they were babies in footie pajamas. I feel like someone sped up the time, and here I was philosophizing about the gospel with grown men who had holy opinions.

In a few minutes, I'll kneel with my husband on our bed for prayer. (Yup, on our bed, not beside it. We are weird.) We'll council about our day and what we think we should pray about, then one of us will talk on behalf of us both to God. The prayers might be repetitious at times. They might be tired and weary, but placed one in front of the other over the span of eighteen years, our nightly prayers have created a comfortable and holy pathway to heaven.

Open your eyes; holiness is in the people around you. It fills your days if you pay attention.

Lest you think all my relationships are the stuff of Hallmark movies and that we all hold hands and sing "Kumbaya," let me burst that bubble right now. Yes, I may be an idealist, but this idealist has lived through some pretty real, raw, and sometimes brutal realities. Relationships aren't holy because they're perfect. They are holy because they are a struggle, and through the struggle, we have the choice to become better, more honest, and more holy.

> Open your eyes; holiness is in the people around you.

This is especially true in our family relationships. We have to work at them to make them work. And we have to have the right expectations for those we love. A very wise person (every time I use the nondescript "wise person" tag, you can go ahead and assume it's my therapist) once told me that dissonance comes when we think our families are supposed to be our saviors and we find them to be incapable of rising to that expectation. Our families aren't our saviors; they're our teachers, and life with our families is our proving ground; therefore, familial relationships will reflect both our best and our worst back to us. To balance this proving ground, sweet President Monson offered inspired council when he advised us to "never let a problem to be solved become more important than a person to be loved."[147] We have the power through the Atonement to

---

147   Thomas S. Monson. "Finding Joy in the Journey," *Ensign*, November 2008.

use the reflections from our familial relationships to change, to grow, to heal. In most situations, we can unite in the journey, and hurt can be repaired as we grow together in our struggles. However, sadly, there are times when relationships should not be repaired. In these times, we lean on the Atonement for healing and understanding, pouring our abundant love into healthier relationships.

How would our relationships change, I wonder, if we would start treating them as the most holy offerings in our lives? At the end of the play *Les Miserables*, the hero, Jean Valjean, is dying. Hovering between heaven and earth, he talks to the Angel Fantine, whose daughter Valjean raised from childhood. Raising this little girl required Valjean to sacrifice everything in his life, and now, at the end of his days, Fantine has come to escort him to heaven. As Valjean faces Fantine and ultimately God, Fantine expresses gratitude to Valjean for raising her child and tells him that his place with God is secure. To which Valjean replies that raising the child was the best thing he had done with his life.

When I think of kneeling before God with my Savior next to me, I think of what I will submit as the best contribution of my life. What will my meager offering in this world be? The relationships I've cultivated rise to the surface of my mind: my husband, children, brothers, parents, extended family, friends, the young women I've served, even strangers I've met. I'm not saying I've done a perfect or even adequate job in my relationships. Certainly, I haven't. But I have loved deeply and offered my whole heart. Love like this is set so far apart from this world, you'll find it in another galaxy. Of everything in life that can be set apart, of everything that is holy, my relationships are the best my life offers.

Chapter Thirteen
writing your holy stories

"And we talk of Christ, we rejoice in Christ, we preach of Christ, we prophesy of Christ, and we write according to our prophecies, that our children may know to what source they may look for a remission of their sins."

—2 Nephi 25:26

My grandmother's handwriting makes me weep. It isn't particularly beautiful. There aren't a lot of feminine swirls and loops. It is unique. Blocky. No nonsense. I love it. Seeing it these many years after her death has the power to take me back to her. I read a label on a number-ten can on which she'd written the word *wheat*, and suddenly I was seven years old, sitting at her counter, eating bottled raspberries from a blue and white bowl while she made bread. After she died, when everything was being divided up in her home, I knew what I wanted. I wanted her pictures and written words. Everything she'd written had a story. I love the piece of paper on which she had hurriedly jotted down a recipe, and I can picture her in a plaid shirt, leaning against the fridge as she wrote it. It brings me joy to read her commentary on a Post-It note attached to the playbill of a production I acted in. As I read it, I am nineteen, seeing past the theatrical fourth wall during curtain call, where she was dressed to the nines and waving. My favorite writings, though, are her letters. My grandmother hoarded letters written to her (and even letters she wrote to her family). When I read my grandmother's letters, I see her as an authentic person who made choices both good and bad, who had great trials and still chose God. Reading her words gives me strength to choose God myself.

The most amazing thing about her papers is what they went through to survive. Life put that woman through the wringer. She didn't have one home. She moved. A lot. She downsized. Upsized. Life-sized. Some of her letters are even caked with dirt from the Teton Dam flood in Rexburg, Idaho, on June 5, 1976. Her home was destroyed. Of all the worldly goods she could have saved, her writings are what she chose. I like to believe she could sense their holiness and the spirituality of writing.

When I write, my words are as much a connection for me to my heavenly family as I hope they will be for my posterity someday. In her book about the power of writing, Julia Cameron says, "We should write because humans are spiritual beings and writing is a powerful form of prayer and meditation, connecting us both to our own insights and to a higher and deeper level of inner guidance as well."[148] When I write, I find myself. I find out what I really think. I see in my writing where God needs me to go.

My favorite T-shirt is emblazoned with the words "YOUR STORY MATTERS." It isn't a very stylish shirt, but I've worn it to the perfect point of softness, and even with all the other

---

148 Julia Cameron. *The Right to Write* [Digital-Kindle], Location 88/3899.

> Our stories and the way we
> tell them will alter what our
> children do with our world
> after we are gone.

actually semi-nice things in my closet, I still reach for it to wear. It's from a conference I attended, hosted by renowned author Donald Miller. After two formative days immersed in the importance of story, I had to buy the shirt, and I've worn it with conviction ever since. I wore it to the top of Table Mountain in Cape Town, South Africa. I wore it as my daughter ran (and lost) for student council. "YOUR STORY MATTERS," it screams in all caps to all the passersby. I hope they listen. Each of our stories is important and needed. Our stories and the way we tell them will alter what our children do with our world after we are gone.

I know that sharing our stories is scary. A couple months after this book is published, you might see me at your local bookstore or at Costco (probably with a scraggly, messy bun on top of my head), the grocery store, or on social media. If you see a normal-looking woman doing her best to smile and be brave while shaking in her animal-print heels, you'll know it's me. Come say hello! I might be nervous to meet you because my stories scare me a little. They make me vulnerable. I have no problem having confidence acting in plays because what I offer on stage is collaborative. A book full of my own stories is a whole different ballgame. If I want you to believe what I am writing, you have to know the real me. I'm not asking you to read a fictional piece of art that another person wrote, another person directed, and another person produced. I am putting my real heart and soul on the table with my innermost thoughts on pages for you to read in hopes that you will, through my stories, hear me saying, "I see you," and find the fortitude inside yourself to make it through another day with joy!

At book signings, I sit among stacks of my own thoughts. Then the scariest, most wonderful thing inevitably happens: someone wants to talk to me. They pick up my book and will usually thumb through it before asking me, "Did you write this book?" Sister, it is so scary. In these moments, I find that the best thing to do is take a deep breath, look into the person's eyes, and try to see part of their story. What do I see in their eyes? Love, pain, hope, joy? Every time, it works. I see you, and when I do, all the fear goes away about you seeing me too.

When I look my sisters in their eyes, I see divinity in stories. My reply is along these lines: "Yes, I did write it. This book is some of my stories. What's one of yours?" In the past two years, scores of women I've met in these situations have shared their extraordinary stories with me. Some were triumphant, some were sad, many were triumphantly sad. Lots of them weren't finished yet. Some had happily-ever-afters. But all of them—all—have been holy. When these women finish telling me their stories, we sometimes stand together awhile and think about what has just been said. These are sacred moments. Quite a few of these women say something like this: "You know, I've always wanted to write a book, to tell my story." With the vigor of all that is inside me, I hope they do.

I hope you do too and that one day I will sit on my favorite reading chair to read your words. I hope your written words will tell me your truth about your heartbreaks and your joys. I want to know the things that made your testimonies shine and also the things that made you question so deeply you considered taking a different path, and why you eventually stayed. I need you to write me stories of hope and love. I need to know where, in the turbulence of your life, you went to find Christ and how He found you back. I need to know how He spoke to you in song lyrics and sent your neighbor over with dinner while you were, long after dinnertime, on your knees, praying for someone to come feed your family. I want my children to know what you did when you thought your prayers weren't answered and what you chose when life didn't go the way you planned.

Can I request one more thing from your writing? Please, when you write your story for us to read, don't edit yourself. When my husband's grandmother was getting older, she asked me to help her type her journals. I was saddened to see so much of what she had written blacked out. She told me they were the "bad" parts about her. She didn't feel safe being her whole self, which was heartbreaking. I'm thankful to see the culture changing. Remember as you write that it is our flaws and imperfections that connect us. Seeing you as flawed and still able to choose Christ will help me choose Him too. Sister, write that book. Tell your stories. Even if no one reads it but you, it is worthy of being written.

I know what you are going to say. That your life is boring. That nothing really happens to you. As my grandma would have said, *hogwash!* I spent a month in Vermont this past summer, and here is what I learned from that glorious month among three-hundred-year-old maple trees: it takes forty gallons of sap in spring runoff to equal one gallon of pure Vermont maple syrup. Forty gallons of sap and hours upon hours of monotonous labor. No one's life is pure syrup. What I need from you is the gallon of meaning and purpose that you boiled down from forty gallons of sap from your life. Or just give me all the sap, and I'll boil it down myself. That's what my grandma did. She gave me hundreds of letters with lots of boring details (which never actually bored me). I read them all. I boiled them down. And what I saw in the holy syrup from her sap was a clear path to Christ. Her voice gives me hope when most of the voices I hear every day are despairing enough to emotionally exhaust me. What if I didn't have these stories? Or the stories of the Saints? All of our stories are important. In the preface of *Saints*, it is noted that "the stories of all Saints, past and present—remind readers how merciful the Lord has been to His people as they have joined together around the globe to further God's work."

If we want to have a voice in the world's narrative, we have to be the ones to write it. In his book *A Million Miles in a Thousand Years*,[149] Donald Miller says, "We live in a world where bad stories are told, stories that teach us life doesn't mean anything and that humanity has no great purpose. It's a good calling, then, to speak a better story. How brightly a better story shines. How easily the world looks to it in wonder. How grateful we are to hear these stories and how happy it makes us to repeat them." Our lives are the "better stories" our grandchildren will someday read in a world we can only imagine them living in. They need us to help them endure just as we lean on the stories of our heritage to survive. Story is the reason we all dress up like pioneers and head to the hills for our trek experiences. Story links us to the past, sending roots of connection deep into

---

149 If you haven't read the book *A Million Miles in a Thousand Years*, go online and order it. Today.

> "And we labor diligently to
> engraven these words upon plates,
> hoping that our beloved brethren
> and our children will receive them
> with thankful hearts."

the earth. How will those who come after know our stories if we don't write them down? How will they find their way?

As a lover of writing and story, I have always loved this scripture in the fourth chapter of Jacob:

> Now behold, it came to pass that I, Jacob, having ministered much unto my people in word, (and I cannot write but a little of my words, because of the difficulty of engraving our words upon plates) and we know that the things which we write upon plates must remain; But whatsoever things we write upon anything save it be upon plates must perish and vanish away; but we can write a few words upon plates, which will give our children, and also our beloved brethren, a small degree of knowledge concerning us, or concerning their fathers—Now in this thing we do rejoice; and we labor diligently to engraven these words upon plates, hoping that our beloved brethren and our children will receive them with thankful hearts, and

> look upon them that they may learn with joy
> and not with sorrow, neither with contempt,
> concerning their first parents. For, for this in-
> tent have we written these things, that they
> may know that we knew of Christ, and we
> had a hope of his glory many hundred years
> before his coming; and not only we ourselves
> had a hope of his glory, but also all the holy
> prophets which were before us.[150]

I love the description of engraving on the plates! It took so much effort on their part to tell their stories. And all we have to do is sit down with a journal and pen or even just download a journaling app on our phone.[151] Tell your story. What you write will remain, what you don't will "perish and vanish away." Our legacies in our stories have the power to become familial scripture that will offer hope to the ones who come after us and can be a form of prayer for ourselves today. I know of Christ, and I have a hope of His glory. May you read this witness in my holy stories, and may I read it in yours.

---

150 Jacob 4:1–4.
151 Day One Journal App.

Chapter Fourteen
"did lay wait to destroy"

"In the premortal Council in Heaven, Lucifer, as Satan was then called, rebelled against God. Since that time, he has sought to destroy the children of God on the earth and to make them miserable."

—Gospel Topics, "Satan"

I am going to tell you an uncomfortable truth: women who seek the holy life open themselves up to an increase in opposition. There isn't a pretty, sweet, or white-tablecloth-on-the-pulpit-during-Relief-Society way to put this. As you increase your desire to live a holy life, you will increase Satan's desire to take you away from it. You, my sister seeking holiness— YOU—are at war. It's an epic battle. And what, then, is the victor's prize? Your one precious and holy life. If the worth of a woman's soul is "great in the sight of God,"[152] so too is the worth of her soul great in the sight of Satan. The lives that will be changed, the influence, the light and goodness of your honest testimony in this world can all be snuffed out if only he can win the prize. He'll even settle for distracting you for a while in his

---

152 Doctrine and Covenants 18:10.

confusing mists of darkness. Anything he can do to delay your progress is a battle won in the ultimate war.

And Satan is not the lone fighter in his quest for you. He and his third part of the hosts of heaven use every tool at their disposal to destroy the holy lives we so carefully carve out for ourselves. Of all the tools Satan uses, perhaps none is more disturbing than his use of other people to aid in our destruction.

In Helaman 2, as an aside to the chapter, Mormon tells us that we are about to meet a dangerously influential man by the name of Gadianton, who is present through many years of history in the Book of Mormon. His evil secret combinations were known and used for generations forward. Mormon says, "And behold, in the end of this book ye shall see that this Gadianton did prove the overthrow, yea, almost the entire destruction of the people of Nephi."[153] But that will come later. In the part we're looking at, it is 50 BC, and this is our introduction to Gadianton, a charismatic and cunning leader of the band of Kishkumen, who did "lay wait to destroy"[154] Helaman and the Nephite people.

It all started well enough. Sure, there was Gadianton and his band of murderers and plunderers, but things were good for the Nephites. In 49 BC, we are told there was "no contention among the people of Nephi."[155] Yet, even then, beneath the façade of peace and prosperity, Gadianton was quietly and stealthily setting his snares of secret combinations to lure away the souls of the righteous Nephite people. His lures were flattery, the offer of fitting in, mixed with a little bit of truth. Within a

153 Helaman 2:13.
154 Helaman 2:3.
155 Helaman 3:1.

few verses, there is more contention. A few verses later, in Helaman 3:23, more peace, "save it were the secret combinations which Gadianton the robber had established." It continues in this pattern, and by chapter 6, verse 31 of Helaman, 25 BC, a mere twenty-four years after "no contention," we read that the Nephites "had become exceedingly wicked; yea, the more part of them had turned out of the way of righteousness, and did trample under their feet the commandments of God, and did turn unto their own ways, and did build up unto themselves idols of their gold and their silver."[156]

The Gadianton robbers and their various leaders remain a fixture in the Book of Mormon until 21 AD, when they are defeated by the repentant and humbled Nephites.

In the end, the Nephites nearly experienced their "entire destruction" and endured seven decades of tumult, brought forth largely by the influence and secret combinations of one man. How can we ever doubt how much one soul is worth?

Gadianton exerted great power, but all of this destruction wasn't his idea! We are told that the "secret oaths and covenants . . . were put into the heart of Gadianton by that same being who did entice our first parents to partake of the forbidden fruit."[157] Yes, even Satan himself! I wonder what Gadianton could have been, don't you? If one man could scheme, destroy, plunder, murder, and influence generations, what good might he have done? It's fitting that Gadianton and his crew were called robbers. Aside from their plundering and stealing, they stole something much more valuable: countless souls who could have changed the world for the better. Other souls and their own.

---

156 Helaman 6:31.
157 Helaman 6:26.

In life, we are faced with our own Gadianton robbers, who, with the voice of Satan in their ears, set out to rob us of our holiness. This sick partnership is one "wrought by men and by the power of the devil, to lead away and deceive the hearts of the people."[158] As we seek the holy life, we need to be aware of the voices in our ears. While the Holy Ghost's voice is small and still, Satan's voice is contrastingly loud and confusing. It isn't always overtly evil, as then we would easily recognize it. It is sly. His is the voice of lies mingled with a little truth.

The voice in your ears that turns you away from light and toward any sort of negativity isn't holy. That is not your voice! That is not God's voice! That is not the Savior's voice! That is not the Spirit's voice! Then whose can it be, whispering to you in the moments when you offer your most vulnerable self, only to have it mocked? Just as God is in the answer to prayer that comes as you watch the autumn leaves fall, or the joy you feel as a gauzy morning mist sets itself down upon the temple spire on your way inside to worship, Satan too is in the details of our lives. He is in the coldness of a thought whispering that you are alone in your sin and unworthiness. He is in the temporary enjoyment and eventual shame in choosing the temptations of the world.

There are two forces at work in this war for the souls of women seeking holiness. Both of these forces are invested in us and in our everyday moments. Our agency decides who influences us. Our discernment reminds us that Satan tells us the worst-case scenario of who we are. And it tells us our Heavenly Family (Father, Mother, Brother Jesus, and the Holy Ghost)

---

158 3 Nephi 2:2.

can show us the best of who we are and who we can be. When we fall short, it is not with shame and scorn that They invite us home. Instead, our Heavenly Parents send forward Their Son to remind us that He already paid the price for you, for me, and for all our accompanying sin, sadness, and heartache. Do we know this? We *must* know this. We must know it so well

> [Christ] already paid the price for you, for me, and for all our accompanying sin, sadness, and heartache.

that in the moment we hear a whispering or feel a feeling that takes us to a place of darkness, we can use the strength we have cultivated to stop and say, "This is not my voice or the voice of anyone who loves me. Those who love me would not speak to me like this." When necessary, cast Satan out!

Our brother Lucifer is just as real as our Savior and is an important part of Heavenly Father's plan of agency. "For it must needs be, that there is an opposition in all things. If not so . . . righteousness could not be brought to pass, neither wickedness, neither holiness nor misery, neither good nor bad."[159]

In the 1986 movie *Labyrinth* (anyone else a David Bowie fan? Just me?), Sarah, a young girl, has just a few hours to save her baby brother from the world of the Goblin King. It's a harrowing adventure in which Sarah initially resists the conflict that arises, refusing to acknowledge the truth of who the Goblin King

---

159 2 Nephi 2:11.

is and his influence in her life. This resistance leads her down a chaotic path full of dead ends and confusion. Finally, though, in one of the classic moments of 1980s

> Satan's interest in our lives is a reality that needs our courageious awareness, not our ignorance.

cinema, Sarah faces reality: the Goblin King is there, and she must stand up to him. As she observes him, she begins to step toward him, and remembering the things she was taught that she would need for this very moment, she looks him in the eye and says, "You have no power over me." The Goblin King, his world, and his power disappear in this one statement of acknowledgment and Sarah's faith in facing him. Sarah finds herself back, safe and warm, in her home.

We don't usually speak of this other brother, Satan. We are afraid. We worry that in acknowledging his power, we add to it. Yet, the act of denying the existence of something does not cause it to cease to be; rather, it often draws undue attention to it, creating confusing "labyrinth"-like journeys in our lives. Sometimes we give Satan more screen-time than he deserves by entering his mazes of lies and deceit. We get lost in the maze when we believe the lies he tells us about ourselves, and we live with shame and self-loathing instead of relying on the Atonement and judging for ourselves. Listening to all Satan has to say can become a never-ending list of ways we get trapped in his labyrinth. Succumbing is the act of simply ignoring his reality and denying ourselves the freedom from his influence that comes with exercising faith in what we have been taught and accessing the power of the Atonement. Satan's interest in our lives is a reality that needs our courageous awareness, not our ignorance.

As you accept the idea that Satan is aware of you and truly fighting for your soul, as you stop resisting the fact that there is a war, you take away the war's power. Accept it. Watch it. Ask for the Spirit to be with you as you say aloud that you are aware of and are observing the conflict. Say aloud that you know Satan is trying you, tempting you, and causing adversity in your life but that you choose Christ instead. As you give voice to the reality, you will watch Satan's influence melt away, and you will be filled with the light you crave. We can bring Satan into the light, where the presence of Christ's Spirit can snuff out that awful darkness and demand him to depart, for light and dark cannot coexist.

It is not uncommon for us to experience a period of intense darkness just before a spiritual awakening. In my own life, I have found it to be true that Satan increases his influence preceding times of great spiritual growth. This darkness can be literal or figurative. It can be a physical manifestation or an internal battle. Being aware of this darkness and even anticipating it will lessen its impact. We can take comfort and courage in stories of prophets, Apostles, and leaders to whom this has happened.

Joseph Smith experienced this in the Sacred Grove. In his history, he says,

> I was seized upon by some power which entirely overcame me, and had such an astonishing influence over me as to bind my tongue so that

I could not speak. Thick darkness gathered around me, and it seemed to me for a time as if I were doomed to sudden destruction. But, exerting all my powers to call upon God to deliver me out of the power of this enemy which had seized upon me, and at the very moment when I was ready to sink into despair and abandon myself to destruction—not to an imaginary ruin, but to the power of some actual being from the unseen world, who had such marvelous power as I had never before felt in any being—just at this moment of great alarm, I saw a pillar of light exactly over my head, above the brightness of the sun, which descended gradually until it fell upon me.[160]

When Hugh B. Brown was first counselor in the First Presidency, he had a remarkable experience. About to come into a great amount of money in his employment, he felt unsettled and felt to call on God to ask about the direction he should take in his life. He went to the mountains to pray, came home, and had the following experience:

I went into that bedroom and closed the door, and I was conscious of a blackness such as I had never known. There was something in that room that made me feel very sincerely that I would like to be rubbed out—that I would like to cease to be. I didn't think of suicide, but I did think seriously that if there were any way that I could be washed out, that would be the best thing that could happen to me.

I spent the night in that attitude, in that aura of awful blackness. Early in the morning Sister Brown came in—she had heard me walking the floor. When she closed the door, she said, "My goodness, my dear! What's in this room?"

I said, "The devil is in this room, and he is trying to destroy me."

Together we knelt at the bedside and prayed for guidance and deliverance. We didn't seem to get it. The next morning I went down to my office in the city. It was Saturday. I knew no one would be there, and I wanted to be alone. I knelt by my cot and pleaded to God for deliverance, for that awful blackness was still on my soul. And it seemed to me that the sun came up. I obtained peace of soul and serenity of spirit.

I phoned Sister Brown and told her, "Everything is all right. I don't know what happened, but it's all right."

That night I was taking a bath. The telephone rang. Sister Brown came to the door and said, "Salt Lake is calling."

I said, "Who in the dickens wants to talk to me at this time of night?" It was 10:30. I went to the phone.

When I said hello I heard a voice that said, "This is David O. McKay calling."

I said, "Yes, President McKay."

"The Lord wants you to give the balance of your life to the Church. Tomorrow will be the closing session of conference. Can you get here in time for the afternoon session?"

I told him I couldn't, as there were no planes flying. He said, "Come as soon as you can."

You know, I didn't think to ask him what there was in it. That's what I would do in an ordinary business deal.

I hung up, and that night—this was the night following the night of blackness in our lives—Sister Brown and I spent another wakeful night, but it was a night of bliss. Not that we were looking for position, but to think that the God of heaven would reach out 1,200 miles and touch a man on the shoulder and say, "Come," and to think that I would be that man was almost more than I could understand!

I told the president when I came down thirty days later about this experience, and he said, "As far as I know, every man who is called into the General Authorities has to wrestle with the devil." You have to have a lot of courage if you come out victorious.[161]

---

161 Hugh B. Brown. *Father, Are You There?* October 8, 1967.

For Hugh B. Brown, the confusion at the direction his life was taking, his praying in the mountains, and an experience with intense darkness preceded the light of being called to the Quorum of the Twelve Apostles and being given his life's direction. If you are seeking a holy life and experiencing an increase in darkness, take heart. The darkness might last a moment or a season, but it will not last forever. You are stronger. Remember that "it is always darkest just before the Day dawneth."[162]

Recognize the experience for what it is, and call upon heavenly help. Get help from others if you need it. And be ready for the increased light that will inevitably follow.

In this humble and Spirit-filled submission, we can lay our burden at the feet of our Savior, and with the strength of Christ's Atonement at our backs, we can "submit [ourselves] therefore to God. Resist the devil, and he will flee from you."[163]

A holy life is honest and unafraid. It isn't afraid to speak truth, and Satan's existence is truth. As he lays in wait to destroy with his modern-day Gadianton robbers, with his temptations, with his legions, and even with his relationship with us before his fall, we stand ready. We are armed with power from on high, testimony, faith, angels, the Holy Ghost, and the Atonement. We are brave, and we are holy.

And because we are holy, the Savior knows us and lays wait to immediately save us. No one can know us better than the person who "[took] upon him [our] infirmities, that his bowels may be filled with mercy, according to the flesh, that he may know according to the flesh how to succor [us] according to

---

162 Thomas Fuller. *A Pisgah-Sight of Palestine and the Confines Thereof* (1650).
163 James 4:7.

[our] infirmities."[164] This faith we have in our Savior and the trust we show in Him when we allow Him to heal even the darkest parts of our lives is what gives us the power to "bruise [Satan's] head"[165] and to proclaim (as is printed on T-shirts and mugs everywhere), "Not today, Satan. Not today."

---

164 Alma 7:12.
165 Genesis 3:15.

Chapter Fifteen
"we barely made it! but we made it!"

> *"Grace is an enabling power that allows men and women to lay hold on eternal life and exaltation after they have expended their own best efforts."*

—Bible Dictionary, "Grace"

This past September, we sold our family property on the Oregon Coast. It was hard, but it was time. One evening before we said goodbye, I sped my tin can of a rental car around the rocky twists of the Pacific Coast Highway, attempting to get to one of my favorite spots for sunset. All along the highway, the blackberry bushes ached to be picked, but I whirled past, leaving them full of sweet berries. I thought the fog would rob me of a sunset that night, but at the last minute, it lifted, leaving me scrambling not to miss the day's last hurrah. A stranger and I arrived at the entrance to the parking lot at the same time. I from the north, and he from the south. He let me pull in first, then he followed. I parked; he parked. I got out; he got out. I was in my teal galoshes. He was in his black ones. Together, we both ran to an overlook along a log fence.

"Whoa," I said, out of breath. "We barely made it."

"We barely made it," he said with a twinkle in his eye before he smiled and said, "but we made it."

Two strangers silently reflected over their separate days, gazing as the sun settled itself into the depths of the Pacific.

Some days it feels like we're barely hanging on and we are anything but holy, but I see myself getting to heaven in the end . . . just in time. Christ and I will rush to a heavenly veil and look back at my life settling itself down like a setting sun.

"Whoa!" I'll say to Christ. "We barely made it!"

"We barely made it," He'll agree, opening His hands, where I'll find myself imprinted in His scars. "But we made it."

As we are ending our time together, my mind races over the many aspects of holiness, even some we didn't address. The holiness of music, of the priesthood power in our lives, of revelation, of faith versus fear, the holy divinity of womanhood itself . . . so many things I wanted us to share with each other and so many words in my heart left unwritten. Yet, that's the point of all of this, isn't it? That every aspect of our lives can be set apart for a sacred purpose? Every facet of our lives can be holy when we see with our spiritual eyes, not our physical ones.

> "We barely made it," He'll agree, opening His hands, where I'll find myself imprinted in His scars. "But we made it."

Your life can be holy every day! Just as in a movie saga where the heroine's quest ends with the knowledge that the answer was always within her, holiness is there inside of you any time you are ready to see it. Be brave enough to be authentically yourself—your individuality is what sets you apart for a sacred purpose! If you are feeling empty and alone, choose to set yourself apart. Invite the awe of your own divine nature into your life. Look at a blade of grass. Listen to a child breathe as they sleep. Embrace your life's significance, then make the changes needed for a more meaningful time in your ordinary, extraordinary existence.

I know there is struggle between the ideal of a holy life and the reality. The two can seem far apart, but I hope this book has helped close the gap with the answer to a question. How is your life different today than it would be if you were not a representative of Jesus Christ; if you had not taken His very name upon you? I expect the answer for you is the same as it is for me: because we belong to Him, everything in our lives is different. Holiness doesn't live solely in a church, a temple, or a place; it lives in us; it lives in you. "And inasmuch as ye have received me, ye are in me and I in you."[166] Sister, your best efforts are enough. You are holy as you are.

---

166 Doctrine and Covenants 50:43.

Post Script
"it is well with my soul"

"Christ hath regarded my helpless estate, And hath shed His own blood for my soul."

—Horatio Spafford

I am writing this book during the pinnacle weeks of autumn in a cliff-faced canyon in Utah. I do a lot of my writing in nature; the normal wrestle I have with the words in my head seems to settle itself into an easy flow when I am amongst God's untouched creations. Any time spent in nature is a gift, but these particular afternoons are just . . . well . . . perfect. The heat of the summer has finally subsided, giving way to those few golden Utah days before one can start to see the coming winter.

Not a soul has found me. The raging spring river has dried to the babble of autumn, making it shallow and calm enough to cross onto a small island in a thicket of tall trees. Here I am hidden, excepting one fisherman who waded past while I was writing yesterday and scared us both to death. With my back pressed against a tall tree, I write about holiness, and I feel the truth of what I write. I feel it in the crispness of the breeze in my hair. The leaves are changing, and an orange butterfly with black spots on its wings, flaps and rests at my feet. If there is anything as close to a temple for me as the temple itself, it is here where the trees exhale so that I can breathe.

> When peace, like a river, attendeth my way, When sorrows like sea billows roll; Whatever my lot, Thou hast taught me to say, It is well, it is well with my soul. Though Satan should buffet, though trials should come, Let this blest assurance control, That Christ hath regarded my helpless estate, and hath shed His own blood for my soul. My sin, oh the bliss of this glorious thought! My sin, not in part but the whole, is nailed to His cross, and I bear it no more, Praise the Lord, praise the Lord, O my soul! For me, be it Christ, be it Christ hence to live: If Jordan above me shall roll, No pang shall be mine, for in death as in life Thou wilt whisper Thy peace to my soul. And Lord haste the day, when the faith shall be sight, the clouds be rolled back as a scroll; The trump shall resound, and the Lord shall descend, Even so, it is well with my soul.[167]

God is in these rocks and in the rickety sigh of aging wood, and here, with my eyes pointed toward the cloudless blue of the sky, I know that God is in me and that I am holy.

---

167 Hymn written by Horatio Spafford in 1876.

Acknowledgments

A writer's work is the product of their life's experiences. Profound thanks go to those who've shared my life and helped to shape my work.

Thank you to the Covenant publishing team for giving me these pages and allowing me to be a part of their story. So many thanks to my editor (and book therapist) Samantha—sweet Sam—Millburn for her encouragement, patience, and talent. This will be three for us, Sam! You've made each one better than I could have ever made it on my own. To Shauna Humphreys for your expert copyediting. To Margaret Weber-Longoria, Christina Marcano, and the graphics department for their gorgeous design work that so perfectly echoes the words in my heart. To Stephanie Lacy for your work on publicity and promotion. To Blair Leishman and Phil Reschke for their work on the audiobook, and to Tammy Kolkman for your work on sales. To Robby Nichols, Verl Sabey, Susan Condie, Doug Gardiner, and all the staff at the Covenant/Seagull corporate offices. So many thanks go to all the retail store managers and retail employees who help share this message with their patrons. I'm so grateful.

To Caitlin Connolly, whose artistic voice speaks to my soul and whose artwork stands next to my written work on the covers of both this and my first book. You speak to women visually in the way I hope to speak verbally. Thank you for being a part of my artistic story.

To my yoga students and fellow teachers at LLYC, as well as my fellow Utah COPA faculty and students. To the young women of the (former) Manila 1st Ward and the leaders I have served with. To my book clubs, women's groups, Relief Society sisters, and friends, my thanks.

Deep thanks go to some of my holy heroes who had influence on this manuscript: Chieko Okazaki, Emma Lou Thayne, Emma Hale Smith, Marjorie Pay Hinckley, Jane Manning James, Belle Spafford, Mother Teresa, Julie B. Beck, Eliza R. Snow, Kate Holbrook, Laurel Thatcher-Ulrich, Phoebe Woodruff, and Sheri Dew.

To the group Protect and Preserve American Fork Canyon, the Pleasant Grove Ranger District, and all the many volunteers who keep American Fork Canyon beautiful. I wrote a large portion of this book at the Martin day-use area, across the river, in a thicket of trees. Every day I went to my "office," sat by my tree, and found the peace I needed to write. Thank you all so much.

Many thanks to our inspired, imperfect, and holy General Authority and auxiliary leaders throughout our history. I read hundreds of talks, articles, teachings, etc., in research for this book. Your words have strengthened, inspired, and challenged me. Thank you for living lives set apart in the best way you knew how to live . . . for being holy—just as you are and were.

To the men and women whose wisdom and stories found their way onto these pages or assisted with specific aspects of this book: Sheila Morrison, Margaret A. Cook, Sarah Granger

Kimball, Cory Atkinson, Anne Bowen, Connie Bennion, David Bennion (in loving memory), Lisa Vermillion Smith, Robert and Erin Axson, John and Chase Hansen, Rebecca Harding, Lindsay Adamson Livingston, Kristin Behling-Valle, Debbie Oborn, Abi Makin, Mason Gardiner, Austin Gardiner, Goldie Axson, Kelsey Kartchner Axson, Ginger Livingston, "Jace," Trisha Tanner, Lindy Taylor, Xiomara Ayers, Kirsten Lunsford, Adrienne Poulsen, Julie Branham, Manila 1st Ward young women, Jaylie Jackson, Chris and Sarah Eager, Mike and Sandi Carter, Amber Gardiner, Helen Gurr, Hailey Gardiner, Elisabeth Gardiner, Christian Gardiner, Doug Gardiner, Scott Livingston, Jake and Heather Carter, Jane Bell Meyer, Suzanne McKay, Diane Schultz, Kathryn Bell, my scriptural sisters, Adrienne Burdette, April Garnett, Julie Webb, Linda Bennion, Cecil and Nina Hansen, Hailey's friends, Jennifer Finlayson-Fife.

Special thanks to Mom, Donna and Rod Gustafson, Michelle Burnham, Allison Books, Holly Richardson, Lisa Newell, Debbie Oborn, Molly Rubert, Stephanie Sorensen, Ganel-Lyn Condie, Kandee Myers, Michelle McCullough, and my stepmom, Mary Axson. Thank you all for all the help with carpools, laundry, cleaning, meals, the well-timed phone calls of encouragement, the kids, being beta-readers, and letting me cry to you in the final weeks of writing and editing this book.

To our dear family: Mom, Dad, Mary, Dad/John K and Mom/Leila. To Robert, Erin, Henry, Ollie, Finn, Goldie, Andrew, Morgan, Tanner, David, Kelsey, Amber, Austin, Mason, Jordan, Annaka, Thomas, April, Conner, Collin, Carson, Kathleen, Sarah, Ben, Annie, Ella, Aunt Kath, and Aunt Diane. And all our loving extended family.

To my own little family, who has sacrificed so much for this book: thank you for your love and your belief in my work. I love and appreciate you. Hailey, Libby, and Christian, thanks for your patience and for being stellar human beings. You make being a mother the "best of my life." Thank you to my husband, Doug—no one has given more for this book than you have. Thanks for walking next to me, hand in hand. Thanks for becoming. For all etenity.

Thanks to my Heavenly Father and Savior Jesus Christ for saving me every day. And finally, to my Heavenly Mother— awakening to your influence, Mother, is like being born and opening my eyes to a love that has always been available to me.

Note: When referring to our Heavenly Parents, I sometimes use the pronoun "Him" or "He," just as we say mankind or fellow man. This is not to say that I believe Deity is exclusively male. "In the heav'ns are parents single? No, the thought makes reason stare! Truth is reason; truth eternal Tells me I've a mother there."[168]

---

168   "O My Father," *Hymns*, no. 292.

About the Author

hristie Gardiner is an author, speaker, trainer, and show host. She is the author of three books, including the best-selling book *You Are the Mother Your Children Need*. Christie enjoys speaking to congregations, where she loves reminding groups of women that with the Savior, they're not alone. Christie is known as an expert in the field of personal development, and her secular training has helped women worldwide find their voices and make a difference in their own unique ways. The charitable arm of her endeavors, Getting Proximate, teaches and encourages people to get close to the most vulnerable members of their communities. Christie's performing career has spanned three decades in theater, television, film, commercials, and voice-over work. She is a longtime faculty member at the Utah Conservatory of Performing Arts (Utah COPA), where she loves inspiring young people to increase their self-esteem through participation in the arts. She also teaches yoga at Lifted Life Yoga Center. In her spare time, Christie can be found in nature or shuttling her children to their activities. She lives in the shadow of a temple in Pleasant Grove, Utah, with her husband, Doug; their three children, Hailey, Elisabeth, and Christian; and their dog, Jack. Become part of the tribe on Christie's website and take advantage of free resources at http://www.christiegardiner.com.

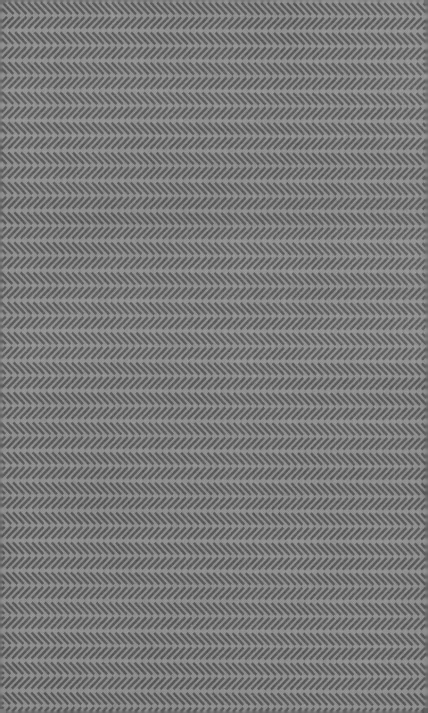